MOTHERING

ANNA MELCHIOR

Mothering

a spiritual and practical approach

ST PAULS

ACKNOWLEDGMENTS

While I alone am responsible for what I have written in this book, many kind souls have helped me to write it. I am particularly grateful to my editor at St Pauls, Annabel Robson, for her terrific good sense and for always saying the right thing; to Sr John the Baptist of the Lamb of God, Fr Dominic Jacob, Leonie Caldecott, Hilary Schlesinger, Fr James Pereiro, and Hyacinth Hickey for showing me the richness of the Catholic faith and supplying me with documents, books, talks, pictures, and poems relevant to it; to Leonie Caldecott also for asking me to present a paper in Oxford in July 2005 under the auspices of *Second Spring* which helped me to define several ideas for this book, her collection of newspaper cuttings, and for reading the manuscript and her comments on it; to Esperanza Arenas de Ballester for inviting me to give a series of talks at Rydalwood, a centre of *Opus Dei* in Manchester, in 2001 from which arose the plan for this book; to Jutta Reimann-Jones and Julia von Gruenberg for support and vision; to Daksha Patel for the photograph of the author; to my husband for proofreading each chapter before I sent it off, and to my children for the joy of mothering them which inspired and inspirits this book.

ST PAULS Publishing
187 Battersea Bridge Road, London SW11 3AS, UK
www.stpauls.ie

ISBN 978 0 85439 728 0

Set by Tukan DTP, Stubbington, Fareham, UK
Printed in Malta by Progress Press Company Limited

ST PAULS is an activity of the priests and brothers
of the Society of St Paul who proclaim the Gospel
through the media of social communication

To my mother, Karin Melchior

Contents

Circles model of mothering

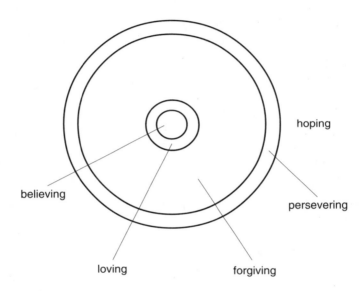

introduction

Our three-year-old has a picture book about a couple of clowns. In the book, the life of the couple of clowns is described. The husband clown leaves their trailer every day to perform his tricks in the circus arena. He stands on his head. He trips and falls over. And he plays a tuba very badly. The spectators laugh, cheer and clap. The wife clown remains in or near the trailer throughout the day and washes and repairs clothes, cleans, and cooks. She listens and talks to their three children and helps the older two with their homework. She cuts the children's hair and plants flowers in window boxes. One day, the husband clown is ill and the circus director at a loss. So the wife clown suggests that she step in and, lo and behold, she, too, can stand on her head, trip and fall over, play a tuba very badly, and make the spectators laugh, cheer, and clap. From that day onward, the wife clown works in the circus arena as well as in and around the trailer.

Now, there is a poignant message for our three-year-old! But I don't think it is what at first you might think it is. I think that the message of the picture book is one which subverts mainstream feminism. The book, you see, is called *Silly Trudie* and the title begs the question whether Trudie is silly before or after she starts standing on her head, tripping and falling over, and playing a tuba very badly, making the spectators laugh, cheer, and clap.[1] That is the question.

However you decide to answer the question for yourself,

the book you are holding in your hands suggests that Trudie had a pretty good job before she started performing antics in the circus arena. I will go into this in greater depth in the first chapter and throughout this book, but would like to share here already my conviction that mothering is an awesome job. Nine months of physical discomfort followed by the most excruciating pain you cannot imagine are only the beginning. Next, and for some twenty years, come the inexhaustible tasks and the countless life-changing decisions which constitute that most fundamental of occupations. Awesome, no doubt – and challenging and fulfilling, I argue, as well.

I love just about everything about mothering. I enjoy organising anything and anybody in my vicinity, and I like sticking to a routine. I get a high from looking at a tidied up lounge and satisfaction out of doing the laundry. I consider the arranging of trinkets an art form and generally look forward to creating order out of chaos in the kitchen, and the standing up whilst washing up aids my digestion, I'm sure. I am proud of my ability to transport the weekly shop on the bike and grateful for the exercise I get lugging the baby around. I take a keen interest in food and find cooking meditative. And if I am honest with myself, I realise that I am actually quite pleased to be unable to spend more thought, time, or money on my appearance (and that I can do my job even when I look like a slob) – I find the certainty that improvement is possible reassuring.[2]

Mothering has great job satisfaction potential. Many women who are mothering derive profound pleasure and pride from various aspects of what they do. And many are, as I was, not a little surprised by the rewards of their job. We are not, after all, engaged in activities generally deemed to confer pleasure or pride. We are not prolonging our youth in youthful carelessness or self-preoccupation. We are not earning certificates, awards, or degrees, and we are not setting records or advancing knowledge. We are not frequenting pubs, bars, restaurants, and health clubs, museums, concert halls, and theatres. We are not creating works of art or literature or music, and we are not travelling the world. We are not bringing home the bacon, and we don't, on the whole, look utterly gorgeous. And yet, there is this creeping satisfaction, this hidden joy in what we do, this deep, consensus-defying knowledge that every act and gesture of mothering is contributing to something that is good.

Mothering, moreover, allows us fantastic freedoms to define what it is about. More than any other occupation, it permits us to express our personality through it and in it rather than despite it or not at all. We do not have to choose whether to fawn or flounder; as mothers, we can be ourselves – and fully human. Our input is key. I am certain that I find mothering so eminently satisfying and fulfilling an activity because I put a lot into it: I learn my life lessons, pursue my interests, and generally grow as a person in and through my mothering, not after hours (just as well, really, as there is no such thing as after hours if you are mothering). If mothering is reduced to the pursuit of convenience, however, and limited to chauffeuring children about, microwaving fish fingers, and turning on a video, it cannot possibly be a rewarding experience. Again, I'll cover this theme in greater depth later on in the book but want to note here that, as with much in life so with mothering, investment pays off. Mothering offers an unrivalled spectrum of challenges and therefore an unmatched richness of experience and learning. It is up to us to make the most of it.

And the thing about mothering is, of course, that we are bringing up our children and isn't it wonderful to be there with them and for them and to see them develop?! And isn't it wonderfully worthwhile to play together with our children and to work together with them, and to teach our children and to learn from them?! So, at the low points – when I stand splattered in poo (why didn't anybody warn me, I wonder, that this could happen while changing a newborn's nappy?), when I struggle through arsenic hour[3], cooking the evening meal while fending off the little ones and barking commands at our big children ("practise, set the table, tidy up, answer the door..."), yes, and when I am interrupted, yet again, as I sit down at my desk to write this ("go away, child, I am writing a book about mothering") – I toss my head of luscious locks, smile, and say "they're worth it"[4]. And, God knows, they are.

Here you are, then, faced with what I like to think of as *radical feminism*. Unlike mainstream feminism, radical feminism values the *roots* of society, which is where mothering – largely unseen – does its essential work. Radical feminism recognises that without sound roots, the rest isn't worth much. Whereas mainstream feminism worries about the glass ceiling, radical feminism worries about the glass floor. It is a fact, after all, that negative prejudice and real as well as perceived economic necessity deny many women and still more men some of the best experiences life has to offer, experiences only accessible to those who spend unhurried time with the children they love. Radical feminism recognises that mothering is an important and difficult as well as, potentially, an incredibly joyful undertaking. Radical feminism, therefore, supports all those involved in mothering, which is exactly what this books seeks to do, spiritually as well as practically.

The meaning of life (1)

This book is not only radical feminist, it is also counter-cultural in a more general sense. I can't help being counter-cultural. Raised by a divorced, employed, American mother in 1970s Germany, I stuck out because of my background and upbringing. I then started to move between cultures (from Germany to Canada to the USA to Ghana to Taiwan to China to the UK) from an early age, never staying long enough to start belonging. To top it off, I studied social and cultural anthropology rather longer than necessary and become somewhat of an expert in cultural difference. What with all of this, I found myself culturally ungrounded. There were few taken-for-granteds left for me: nearly everything was open to doubt, to questioning. Thank God (literally), I managed to swing by apathetic perplexity. I have, in addition, found by now my rather prolonged stay in England and my marriage to an Englishman to have had a remarkably settling effect on me. The exhaustion that comes with mothering may have helped, as well.

At any rate, my doubting and my questioning and my going against the prevailing current are quite tame these days. I doubt, for example, the necessity of a daily bath for young children. And I question the advisability of the common English custom of separating children's mealtimes from adult mealtimes. I see absolutely no reason not to let toddlers handle proper cutlery (our one-year-old enjoys playing with a knife and fork while sitting at table). And I don't think that children should have much say in deciding what foods they eat. I would if I had my way entirely (I don't, incidentally) banish television and computer games from our household and never ever buy a branded item of clothing. I have often left our older children (ten and twelve) in charge of the younger ones (one and three), without feeling either guilty or worried about it. And I would, but for frequently exercised self-control, reprimand other people's children exactly as I reprimand my own whenever I considered it necessary. I have a pet hate for prams which I consider unsuitable for babies (I used a pram for my shopping once, and that worked well), and I think bottle feeding a bizarre custom. I spend an hour or so most week nights cooking (my husband cooks on week-ends), and keep all leftovers. I adore cabbage.

Such are some of my tame counter-cultural idiosyncrasies (which are, I'd like to point out, all quite conventional *somewhere*). Fortunately, I have found that a counter-cultural approach to mothering has significant advantages. It means that you can re-invent mothering for yourself. It means that you can be eclectic about the advice and examples you follow. A counter-cultural approach frees you from rehashing your own upbringing or parroting currently prevailing patterns. Instead, it encourages you to examine critically local habits and to look around for inspiration not only next door, but also in the next country, and the next. And the good thing about that is that by looking around you can appreciate the variety of possibilities and, with that, the variety of reasons for mothering in this way or another. And that gets you to think about mothering and to see it continually in a new light which makes the job forever fresh and interesting and challenging. Furthermore, if you look at mothering practice further afield, you are likely to find support for that controversial gut feeling you had had all along about some central aspect of mothering, and that, in turn, gives you greater confidence to find your own way. So the next time well meaning relatives inquire whether you are really still breastfeeding, you can retort that, yes, you are, and well under the world average of four and a half years, too!

I don't suggest that you keep revising your mothering methods or go entirely against the norms of the society in which you live ("today, children, I'll bring you up the Ghanaian way and you can all miss school to help me with the chores"⁵), but would like to encourage you to question conventions and be open to unconventional input. The counter-cultural approach is a mix of scepticism and curiosity which enables you to discover for yourself what suits you and your family best and to develop your mothering as you go, rather than accept anything ready-made. The counter-cultural approach makes mothering a much richer and more rewarding experience.

While radical feminism runs through the book like a steady stream – I wouldn't have written it if I had not been convinced of both the value and the joy of mothering – the counter-cultural approach provides the occasional refreshing

14

shower, inviting you to see mothering from a new angle or two.

The meaning of life (2)

This book is not only radical feminist and counter-cultural, it is also Christian. You may be inclined to think that radical feminism, counter-culture, and Christianity make odd bedfellows. I suspect, however, that you cannot get more radical feminist or counter-cultural[6] than Christianity these days! Even so, Christianity did not come to me easily.

I was raised an atheist, and an arrogant one at that. In my childhood home, all religions, and Christianity in particular, were put in a drawer marked 'uninteresting' and 'crutch' – a judgment based, to be sure, entirely on ignorance as there is little, if anything, more interesting or more challenging nowadays than to have and live a faith. As I remember it, it was my realisation at university that I could convincingly argue the case for any course of action whatsoever that prompted my interest in religion. If I could not rely on my reason to guide me, as it evidently followed wherever my desire led, where else could I turn? At the age of nineteen, therefore, I peeped into the drawer.

Together with a group of similarly interested students from my American college, I sat still and silent for hours in a Buddhist meditation centre, shared a weekend with the bearded men and kerchiefed women of a Bruderhof community, enjoyed great food and discussions with adherents of the Bahai faith, and got up at 4 a.m. for an Easter sunrise mass celebrated by Benedictine monks – wonderful! – followed by a gorgeous breakfast, also wonderful.

What initially impressed me most, apart from the food, was that – surprise, surprise – there was such a number of people who were both highly intelligent and religious.

How could that be, if religion was an uninteresting crutch? Well, maybe it wasn't, and those highly intelligent religious people had something to teach me. And so I began to ask questions and to listen. One friend, who today is an overworked nun in a silent order, had an especially great influence on me. I have yet to come across a keener mind and a profounder faith. She was easy-going and kind, but also extremely focused and intolerant of claptrap. And she was a recent convert to Catholicism. My desire to become a Catholic was born of our endless conversations.

And so I set out on the path. One thought, in particular, kept me going: I wanted to have a faith to pass on to my children when I became a mother; I wanted my children to be able to know a faith and derive benefit from it, a fundamental human experience which had been denied me as a child. My desire to become a Catholic waxed and waned and waxed again. It outlasted several changes of country and boyfriend and instructions in the Catholic faith by three different priests. It soon became clear to me, however, that my conversion was a course of action that wasn't mine alone to decide. I wanted faith, after all, and faith is a gift. So I waited.

And then the gift came to me, in a peculiar and peculiarly appropriate way. My road to Damascus[7] lay in Taiwan and I was running on it for exercise when, all of a sudden, I was overcome by an overwhelming sense of the presence of God. For a few minutes, if that, I *knew* God was everywhere. I looked at the trees and knew God was in the rustling leaves. A lorry was pulling away ahead of me, and I knew God was in the smelly exhaust. This last one clinched it for me. (I am environmentally rather concerned, you see, and had never been able to look upon exhaust as anything but disgusting, poisonous fumes.) The gift I had been waiting for had been given to me.

As it happened, it happened just in time. A year and a half later I was married, less than two months after my reception into the Church. And ten months after the

16

wedding, our first child was born. I had a faith, and I could pass it on.

The gift had been given to me, but it was up to me to use it. My confessor at the time helped me to understand the important parallels between having a faith and having a husband! The gift of faith just as the gift of love between spouses, needs application to stay alive and effective; it needs, in other words, putting into practice even when – or, rather: especially when – it seems more like a dim memory than an overwhelming sensation. Faith, like love, is an operative principle or nothing: to continue to exist, to change and to grow, it has to translate into action.

And there you have the source as well as the destination of all the currents in this book. In this book, I look at mothering as *faith in action*. Mothering, I argue, is best understood as the continual application, testing, and deepening of our faith. This understanding of mothering carries enormous benefits for the practice of mothering. When understood as faith in action, the many-layered significance of every act of mothering becomes apparent. When mothering is understood as faith in action, moreover, a not only time-tested but divine (!) guide to mothering accompanies us through the trials and triumphs of mothering. And, what is still more, the benefits are mutual: while our faith enriches our experience of mothering, our mothering enriches our faith. When mothering is understood as faith in action, therefore, every act of mothering offers us the opportunity to develop as Christians. It offers us, in other words, the chance to grow in holiness. And there is a great need for that. And fantastic joy in it, too.

Meanings

A few words about words. I am using the word *mothering* because its meaning is more comprehensive than that of the term *parenting* which generally refers mainly to the socialisation of children. I am not using the word *fathering* because in customary usage it denotes altogether too brief an effort to warrant a book about it. I prefer the expression *mainly mothering* to the term *full-time mothering* because it is more flexible and hence inclusive and because it represents a more accurate reflection of most women's actual practices and preferences.[8] The expression also avoids the sharp distinction commonly drawn by our language and our politicians between so-called full-time mothers and so-called working mothers which sets up a false and most unhelpful dichotomy. For brevity's sake, I will in what follows refer to those who are doing the mothering as *mothers*, realising full well, however, that many who are engaged in mothering are not mothers at all, but fathers, grandparents, aunts, uncles, friends of the family, or professional carers.[9] Having said that, however, my use of the word *mother* acknowledges the facts that most mothering is done by mothers and that there are aspects of mothering which only mothers can experience.

The first chapter of this book, *mothering*, focuses on the job of mothering in all its importance and complexity; it is at once a job description and a pep talk. Show it to your husband/friend/neighbour in full paid employment and they'll treat you with reverence in future (should do, anyway). The first chapter also introduces the model of mothering which I use in this book to distinguish and relate the different aspects of mothering. The second chapter, *believing*, looks at the spiritual aspect of mothering. It suggests that God is both an ideal foundation for mothering and the perfect model of mothering. Chapter three, *loving*, is concerned with the emotional aspect of mothering. It explores how God's love for us can feed as well as guide our love for our children. The fourth chapter, *forgiving*, considers the social aspect of mothering. It discusses the art of forgiveness and the setting of rules, and looks once more to God as a model to emulate in the pursuit of both. The fifth chapter, *persevering*, examines the practical aspect of mothering. It points to a number of ways of meeting the challenges entailed in managing a home and family. The sixth and final chapter, *hoping*, offers a summary of the preceding chapters, a vision of the future of mothering, and a call to action. It explores how the different aspects of mothering – believing, loving, forgiving, and persevering – work together and depend on each other and proposes changes to society which will help us all to believe, to love, to forgive, and to persevere.

The purpose of this book is to help with mothering. I see little point in only talking about mothering and not offering to help! Whatever age your children are, and whether you mainly mother or mainly do something else, and whether or not you are a Christian, I hope to engage you in reconsidering the job of mothering from several different and hopefully helpful perspectives. I also offer plenty of practical suggestions which I and others have found helpful, in case you'll find them helpful, as well. And if you are not mothering yet, read on, as there is nothing like being prepared for the job. And if you prefer to let others do the mothering for you, I'd also urge you to read on as it is very important to have a good understanding of what it is you are delegating. And if you are not mothering now and do not plan to, read on, as well, because the mothering mothers do involves and affects everyone of us.

NOTES

1 My translation of the original German, *Die dumme Augustine.* A clown is, of course, supposed to be silly.

2 The problem with makeovers from this perspective is that they supposedly leave you looking the best you can possibly look. If that isn't that great, where then do you turn for reassurance?

3 An American friend introduced me to this term for the hour or so before the evening meal is ready.

4   The reference is to a L'Oreal advertising campaign in which the lusciously locked model endorses a product "because you're worth it". The other, significantly less profound, thought that helps to keep me going at these times is that our children actually are a troupe of comedians doing their best to amuse me. And they do.

5   Even so there is a lesson here, albeit one we can only whisper in the UK: there are more important things in a child's life than attending school.

6   Fr Ronald Rolheiser sums up the situation: "In the Western world today, the only intellectually sanctioned bias is that against Roman Catholicism and Evangelical Protestantism. To be bigoted here is not interpreted as intolerance or as being narrow-minded. Rather it's seen as the opposite, a sign that one is enlightened and liberal", *The Catholic Herald*, 12 September 2003.

7   Jesus spoke to Saul as he was travelling to Damascus, intent on persecuting Christians. Saul, of course, became St Paul. We're not holding our breath, however, concerning my future development.

8   Most women want to give *priority* to the needs of their children, cf. Catherine Hakim, *Work-Lifestyle Choices in the 21 Century* (Oxford: Oxford University Press, 2000).

9   Some of the best mothers I know are men.

1
mothering

This book aims, above all, to be useful. In practice, there is little more useful than a positive attitude to the task at hand, be it writing a book, managing a company, or bringing up children. I begin, therefore, by examining attitudes to mothering – and grounds for improving them.

Mothering has in some respects become more difficult in recent decades. The difficulties mothers face today are psychological as well as practical, and stem from the increasingly problematic interface between mothering and the rest of society. The government promotes a Brave New World of institutionalised childcare. The economy promotes long working hours and the flexibility to travel and move for a job. The education system promotes measurable achievement. The media promote glamour and un-committed sex. Advertisers promote eternal youth and consumption. And all of these – the government, the economy, the education system, the media, advertisers – promote the prime importance of income to our sense of who we are.

Mothering does not fit any of these agendas. Mothers are generally convinced that they do a better job of bringing up their children than professionals who do not love and, if the childcare setting is large, barely know the children they care for. Mothers resent demands on themselves or their husbands to put work before the family. Mothers cannot be rated, graded, quality-assessed; there are no certificates, no awards for mothers. Mothers rarely manage to look glamorous. Mothers are emblems of the reproductive function of sex and the need for committed relationships. Mothers quite literally embody adult responsibilities, and hence expose the fiction of eternal youth. Mothers, almost by definition, give rather than take, and, as a result, have little to show for the way they spend their time. Mothers, finally, are not paid for the work they do, and therefore find themselves at the bottom of the prevalent status scale coping with a precarious sense of self.

Mainstream feminism is no help. Mainstream feminism has become a pawn of the forces that shape society. Its goals conform perfectly to the agendas listed above, agendas which have prestige, power, and profit as their object, not the welfare of women. Although most mothers of small children would like to give priority to the needs of their children and many career-oriented young women change their minds in favour of mainly mothering once they have children[1], the women with whom mainstream feminism concerns itself are not women who choose to mother[2]. As a result it is now, for example, un-PC to suggest that children need mothers who have time for them and that mothers, at the very least, need husbands who can support them emotionally, practically, and financially.

Mothering tends to be an invisible activity producing immeasurable outcomes. Our society is attached to the visible above the invisible and to the measurable above the immeasurable and thus cannot cope with mothering. We therefore try to ignore mothering, pushing mothers further into the realm of the invisible. As a result of this vicious circle, we generally do not know much about mothering unless we ourselves become mothers and easily under-estimate what mothering involves. The writer Deborah Jackson notes that "great and valuable efforts are spent preparing the pregnant woman for the actual Birth Day [...] but few urban women are prepared – emotionally, physically, or practically – for the arrival of babies themselves".[3] To improve attitudes towards mothering, therefore, we must first of all look at what this most underrated of vocations is actually about.

The work of mothering

A friend once remarked while we were still at school that she didn't really mind what job she got later on as long as it required her to wear a suit. I laughed. Since becoming a mother, however, and occasionally enduring suit-yearnings, I have thought about my friend's statement more seriously. A suit conveniently indicates status. The suit wearer is thought to have special skills. The suit wearer is thought to have power over other people. The suit wearer is thought to make money. Obviously, not everyone who enjoys the status that special skills, power, and an income confer wears a suit. Nonetheless, the suit has become a marker and symbol of what society values – hence my friend's succinct expression of her hopes for her working life.

Mothers don't wear suits. And there lies the rub. Mothers are thought to have no special skills. Mothers are thought to have no power over people. Mothers are thought not to make any money. Mothers therefore suffer from low status in our society. At worst, they are regarded as living fossils and curious reminders of a remote and very different past, or pariahs who present a threat to the dominant values of society. Their low status seems to leave mothers only two alternatives: either they start wearing suits and leave the mothering to others, or they keep their heads down and try not to draw attention to themselves. Jill Kirby, who chaired the *Full Time Mothers* network, once suggested that mothers register as childminders and swap children. They would then be deemed to be 'working' and receive financial support as well as recognition from the government.[4] Mothers could even don suits when the social services inspectors came to visit. But there is a genuine third alternative: mothers can reject the low status society has bestowed upon them and claim the recognition and support they are due.

Mothering is not about wasting your genius in domestic drudgery. Mothering is about loving, educating, and managing; it is about enormous challenges, responsibilities, and freedoms. Mothering is about being resourceful and resilient. Mothering is about applying diverse skills to diverse problems, constant decision making, and multitasking. Mothering is about using your genius.

Let us look specifically at the notion that mothering does not require special skills. As a matter of fact, there are many challenges involved in mothering and therefore a corresponding number of skills required of the mother.

As a mother, you have to define your job and set your goals yourself. You have to determine for yourself the fundamental meaning and purpose of your job, its broad overall objectives, and its daily targets. And, more often than not, you have to do all this in isolation from others facing similar challenges. Even top executives rarely shoulder such profound and diverse responsibilities, and certainly not on their own.

It is easy to get thrown by this particular challenge because the importance of what you are doing when you are mothering is so great, and yet mothering is made up of so many seemingly unimportant tasks. You are not taking big steps – signing big cheques, addressing huge crowds – to achieve big things. As a mother, you achieve big things little by little, and it is not always easy to keep the long-term goals (communicating your values to your teenager, for example) in the short-term picture (getting him to help with the washing-up this evening). If a mother was an organisation, that organisation would have several levels of management!

As a mother, you have to engage your whole self – spiritual, emotional, intellectual, physical – in what you do for up to twenty-four hours a day. Paid work is to mothering as communication via e-mail is to a face-to-face conversation: you can withhold part of yourself, present only a selected self in a controlled fashion, and withdraw to a separate realm of privacy. Colleagues let you do that, children don't. Offices empty at night, homes remain full of life.

When your toddler wakes you up at 3 a.m. to ask you whether monkeys eat light bulbs (true story, though not mine), you face not only the physical effort of rousing yourself from sleep and bed but also the emotional and intellectual challenge of responding appropriately to her earnest inquiry and settling her back in her bed. All the while you are facing as well, of course, the amazing mystery that is the toddler mind.

As a mother, you have to manage many extremely diverse situations, often simultaneously. You have to manage people in all their complexity, ever-changing logistical requirements, usually sparse money, and a household. Mothers, moreover, have to be able to manage all this with the flexibility befitting an Olympic gymnast.

When the builder you hired is on the roof and the cake in the oven while your son is practising the violin and you are doing the ironing and listening to your daughter's complaints about her teacher as a friend rings to ask whether she can drop off her toddler because she has to take her baby to the doctor's surgery, you don't need anyone (just then, anyhow) to tell you that mothering requires management skills.

As a mother, you have to acquire and use knowledge of a wide range of subject areas. You have to learn quickly and independently about matters as diverse as nutrition, child development, and plumbing. There is no ultimate handbook for mothers as mothers constantly encounter new and different challenging situations and demands to which they have to respond – now. The world of work is by comparison, as G.K. Chesterton put it, "a madhouse of monomaniacs".[5] There are few other jobs that require as broad a knowledge base and regularly call upon it with similar urgency.

When we decided to get our loft converted a few years ago, I obtained quotes from ten different builders and interviewed each one about the job. Every interview taught me something about the processes and the possibilities involved which, in turn, enabled me to assess the skill and understanding of the builders as well as to refine our requirements, supervise the work being carried out, spare us disappointment, and save us thousands of pounds. This is an example of on-the-job learning that is incidental to mothering and which I, as you will have gathered, enjoy hugely.

Finally, mothering is the one job from which you cannot walk away. Mothers therefore need the ability to persevere.

So much for the idea that mothering does not require special skills. You cannot acquire these skills at university or through distance learning. Mothers learn them by applying themselves to the tasks their job entails. Fortunate indeed the country or organisation that can enlist experienced mothers!

What about the idea that mothers do not have any power over people? This perception is also wide of the mark. The power that mothers wield is not specified in a constitution or a company charter but is, nonetheless, considerable. Society as well as mothers themselves need to recognise this fact so that society can support mothers in the use of their power, and so that mothers can use their power with deliberate purpose.

As a mother, you are the most important person in your child's life. You give your child love, security, and values. Without these, children cannot develop into well-adjusted adults. Mothers make men and women.

I remember holding our children as babies and realising that I held an awesome power as well as a great responsibility. I did not find this realisation daunting, but then I had a supportive husband and family as well as economic security to hold me as I held the babies. Husbands and families, politicians and employers make mothers.

As a mother, you are the centre of the home, which is the base and refuge of the family. In the home, the family – without fear of rejection – learn and never stop learning what it means to be human: what it means to share their selves with others. The home, moreover, is the place where the family come to rest and recharge and be reassured, whether after a morning at nursery or a trip abroad. If we lack time among those who know, love, and accept us, it is easy for us to lose track of who we are. And that makes us vulnerable. Studies indicate that marriage and families are good for mental as well as physical health.[6] Families let society function.

As a mother, you create community. It is mothers taking care of the three C's – children, church, and chores – who guarantee that there is such a thing as community. It is mothers helping each other with childcare, mothers discussing the skills of teachers and handymen, mothers taking turns with the children's liturgy at church, mothers looking after sick or elderly relatives and neighbours, and mothers shopping locally who create community. What, if anything, would 'community' mean if everyone worked somewhere else from nine to six?[7]

Community, like mothering, requires both quality and quantity time. The occasional intense burst of effort, on the governing body of the local school, for example, is, of course, very much worthwhile but not in itself the backbone of community. Community, like mothering, is essentially a continuous conversation about whatever happens to come up.

As a mother, you are the foundation of society. By having children, you keep society going. By raising your children well, you make society better. By caring for children, making a home, and creating community, you give society meaning and value.

A childless professional once claimed that his (her?) dog was just as valid a reason to get off work early as someone else's child.[8] Is it? Christian perspectives[9] aside, the point remains that pets – however dear to their owners – are not essential to society. It is therefore not in the interest of society to grant special rights to their carers. Children, on the other hand, are the beginning and the end of society. Without them, we are going nowhere.

As a mother, you support the economy. Half the British economy consists of unpaid work largely done by mothers.[10] It is this vast amount of unpaid work which enables the other half of the economy to carry on as it does, with employees working five long days a week away from the care of the young, the sick, and the elderly.[11] In addition, the production and co-operation taking place in families adds, it has been estimated, at least one-hundred per cent to the value of purchased goods.[12] The value of food and clothes, for example, and of the home itself increases through the work of mothers. Mothers' purchasing decisions on behalf of their families, moreover, help to determine the success or failure of businesses and brands, impact on broad economic trends, such as organic food production and fair trade, and have a significant effect on areas of political as well as economic concern, such as the health of the nation. This last point is my particular baby. In fact, I want to shout it from the roof tops:

Mothers: we are carrying a heavy burden –
let's carry that burden some place good!

If mothers were to quit mothering today, we would soon live in a poorer, ageing population of maladjusted homeless adults and face the collapse of our communities and the economy. The world will go on without bankers, doctors, politicians, scientists, and teachers. But not without mothers. The power of mothers is awesome.

That is all very well. Mothers, however, do not make any money. And without their own income, they are pitiable dependent creatures. Or so current opinion would have it. But let us examine the notion of independence with respect to mothering and other jobs.

28

As a mother, you define the specific nature of your job. You are childcare expert, catechist, tutor, psychiatrist, nurse, nutritionist, manager, chef, entertainer, and ethical consumer to the extent *you* deem appropriate or necessary. You can, in addition, choose to be chronicler, chess coach, gardener, interior decorator, property developer, fund-raiser, bee keeper, seamstress... you name it.

The possibilities inherent in mothering are endless and endlessly changing as your family grows and contracts and as you develop different interests and confront different needs. While the tasks of mothering require plenty of creative input, setting and re-setting the parameters of mothering itself presents an even greater creative challenge.

As a mother, you decide the why, what, when, and how of your working life. You don't have a superior who imposes their values, goals, timetables, standards, and controls on you.

You are your own boss when you are mothering. As boss, you still have to listen, negotiate, and compromise, of course, but you are ultimately answerable only to your own conscience.

As a mother, working with the children you love as you think best, pursuing your goals within the timetable you have set yourself, you suffer from no fundamental doubts about the value of the work you do.

Which other job is as obviously valuable at all times? Due to their dependence on external factors, even professionals can rarely respond to their clients' needs as they would wish to and furthermore are obliged regularly to spend significant periods of time documenting and justifying their activities.

As a mother, finally, you can spend time with your children when they need you. Few other jobs give you that freedom.

This is, perhaps, the most necessary freedom of all: the freedom to spend time with loved ones. Poverty can deny mothers that freedom, but so can the pursuit of prosperity.

The independence of mothering, once you are used to it, is very difficult to give up – even for financial independence.[13]

Mothers, albeit suitless, evidently need many and diverse skills and wield considerable power over individuals and families as well as, collectively, over communities, society, and the economy. Mothers, moreover, enjoy remarkable independence from external impositions and interference. The denigration of mothering, therefore, has nothing to do with the job as such but with ignorance as well as, I suspect, with fear of the awesome challenges, responsibilities, and freedoms that come with the job – challenges, responsibilities, and freedoms from which many choose to escape into the office.

Mothering, then, does rather well when assessed by the standards of other challenging, important, and rewarding occupations. Mothering is, however, far more fundamental and significant an occupation than all these others, save one.

We all are familiar with images of the Madonna and Child. There is God made man, made baby, in fact, small and vulnerable, held in his mother's arms. There is Mary, the one without sin who at first did not understand but who said "yes" anyway to the will of God, holding the infant. And there is, indeed, the foundation of our faith and of the Church: our Lord and our Lady, neither of whom would have been without the other. There are, as well, the definitive exemplars of men and women: priest and mother. Men are called to be priests like Jesus and women are called to be mothers like Mary, some literally and others in an extended sense.[14] Both roles: priest and mother, are fundamental to our communities. Both, priests and mothers, give us hope and life. While priestly functions tend to place men under the gaze of many, motherly functions tend to place women in the background.[15] As priests break the bread at the altar, mothers are standing in the aisles[16], holding their babies. Bread and babies, life and hope.

The image of the Madonna and Child thus sums up much Catholic teaching. It also acts as a powerful corrective to the sort of feminism that would have the imitation of man be the salvation of woman. Being centre stage and in the spotlight can be glorious and is essential for getting certain important jobs done. Being in the wings, beyond the spotlight, can also be glorious and is definitely essential for getting certain important jobs done. Mary's quiet "yes" to God's plan for her would not have made headlines. Her caring for Jesus who, when not serenely looking at us, needed no doubt to be cuddled and played with and washed and changed and fed and soothed, did not attract admirers. And yet she worked for our redemption in her attitudes and actions. Mary's example helps us to recognise the "transcendental importance of an apparently unimportant life".[17] And in following Mary's example, in assenting to God's will as well as in mothering, we give our life transcendental value. "If the Christian woman [had] the courage to live the faith today, in its full dimensions [...] there would be a total turn about in what today is looked upon as success and good fortune"[18] – and the salvation of woman, as well as of man, would be that much closer.

The nineteenth-century educational philosopher Pestalozzi noted that a child's idea of God is based on the child's experience of mothering. A child who has been mothered well, whose needs have been met and who has been loved with warmth, understanding, and respect, can develop trust and faith in a loving God. A child who has been neglected, on the other hand, will struggle with the idea of a loving God. In a very real sense, then, mothers lay the foundation of the faith of the next generation and therefore of the future of the Church. "The history of every human being passes through the threshold of a woman's motherhood: crossing it conditions 'the revelation of the children of God'".[19] Through our mothering, we generate and nurture life for the building of the Kingdom of God and spread the Gospel of a loving, just, and merciful God.

Long before I married, it was the fashion among my set of precocious teenage cynics to decry the idea of having children on the grounds that the world was such a terrible place, "You wouldn't want to bring children into this mess, would you?" To which I replied, with curious confidence, that my children would help to make this world a better place. I still believe that.[20] The call to motherhood is the call to change the world for the better. Nothing less. As Mary holds the Christ Child, we hold up the image of Christ to our family and to society in every task we perform as mothers. Carrying our baby, for example, is an act of devotion to the preciousness of God's gift of life. In comforting our child after an upsetting experience, we communicate God's love. And when we overcome our anger and deal gently with our teenager's misbehaviour, we reflect God's mercy towards sinful humanity. Thus equipped – with a vivid sense of God's gift of life, God's love, and God's mercy – our children will make this world a better place.

Working mothers

Obviously, all mothers are working and, what should have become clear from the above if it was not already, mothers who mainly mother often work very hard indeed. Here, I approach the subject of 'working mothers' as commonly understood, however, and indicate the general background and direction of my thinking on some of the issues involved. I return to the topic from a variety of angles throughout the book.

My own journey to mainly mothering was not straightforward. When I first became a mother, I found it difficult to discriminate between the various views on mothering coming at me and to make decisions about something I hardly knew anything about – and I did not know much about mothering until I had been in the thick

32

of it for quite some time. Our first two children, born within eighteen months of each other, attended crèche in the mornings from a very young age (nine months and nearly seven months, respectively). I was writing my thesis and was hooked on swimming several times a week, and I wanted the mornings to do my work and to get my exercise. I liked those mornings off mothering: they gave me time on my own as well as a foothold in my old life, and probably helped me to enjoy mothering more than I would have done had I suddenly given up my student-identity altogether. I was, moreover, eager to live up to expectations that I was not about to forsake my supposed calling in life for something as banal as mothering. But my heart was at home. When our second batch of children came along several years later, I consciously, and with some trepidation, embarked on a career of mainly mothering. And I am still at it – this book notwithstanding (I am writing this sentence as the two little ones are bouncing on the bed beside me) – and grateful for very nearly every minute in my job.

It now strikes me that the public and political discussion on working mothers labours under a fundamental flaw. The discussion is premised on the assumption that the economy is society's greatest asset and that, therefore, families must fit their lives around the requirements of the economy. However, society's greatest asset is the family. It is in the family and through the experience of being mothered that children feel themselves loved and learn to love themselves and others. It is in the family and through the experience of being mothered that children develop values that will support them and guide them throughout their lives. It is in the family and through the experience of being mothered that children learn to share responsibility and to work with others towards a common goal. The best childcare setting cannot achieve what mothering in the average family achieves as a matter of course. It takes mothering and family life to teach children life's fundamentals. We therefore need to stop fitting family life around the requirements of the economy and begin to fit the economy around the requirements of family life.

The public and political discussion on working mothers also considers it a truism that mothers need more and more affordable childcare. They don't. Of course, a very small minority of mothers who cannot meet the demands of mothering themselves need affordable childcare of a very high standard, and money and effort must go towards meeting this need. Ideally, however, these women should have received help long before they became mothers. (Perhaps greater support for *their* mothers would have prevented much sorrow.) In the public and political discussion on working mothers, this urgent need for childcare and the economic need for childcare are generally fused, which greatly hinders constructive and creative thinking on the matter.[21] The vast majority of mothers do not need more childcare: they need more time with their children. To enable mothers to spend more time with their children, the tax system needs to be restructured so as to benefit families and more flexible (in terms of hours as well as location), rewarding, and secure part-time jobs must become available which allow mothers (as well as fathers!!) to care for their children themselves. In addition, structures are needed to facilitate returning to work after years, rather than months, of mainly mothering. Back-to-work courses and seminars would be helpful as would, more generally, appreciation of the many skills and competencies acquired by mothers through mothering. The determination and effort required to restructure the tax system and the work place will be repaid a thousand-fold by the benefits gained by absolutely everybody in society when mothers are given time to mother as well as by the advantages gained by employers when they harness the talents of experienced mothers.

Before you decide to take on work that takes you away from your child,[22] therefore, consider the following questions.

34

How old is your child? What are your child's particular needs? And how many hours do you propose to leave your child in childcare? The overwhelming consensus of child psychologists is that very young children develop best when they have their mothers at home with them most of the time. Playgroups are beneficial childcare settings, however, because they give mothers a break, introduce small children to other children and other adults, and because they supplement mothering rather than try to substitute for it. Older children are often also in great need of reassurance from their family and from familial surroundings. In addition, all children, irrespective of age, thrive on periods of off-time spent in their own homes (provided the television and the computer remain switched off), which give them a chance to recuperate, process learning, and develop their independence as they figure out themselves what to do with themselves.

Do you know someone who is able to look after your child almost as well as you? Unless you are lucky enough to have a caring relative or friend or a good childminder able to take on your child for part of the day, the answer to this question is almost certainly no – the reassuring palaver about early years curricula[23] and after-school-club activities notwithstanding.

To what extent does your family depend on your income, and could you raise the necessary money in some other way? Downsizing or letting a room are options for home-owners. Doing without a car, buying fewer things and mostly second-hand, as well as taking holidays closer to home are also possibilities. These strategies incidentally have the added and significant advantage of reducing damage to the environment and slowing global warming! Don't forget to subtract the financial cost of working (childcare, commuting, work-clothes, convenience foods) from your prospective income when you do your sums.

How much do you enjoy your job and what about it do you enjoy – the work itself, the status, the money, the time

35

away from home? It is helpful to be wary of adopting as your own the convictions of others as to who you should be. It is also helpful to be prepared for your priorities to change radically through the experience of mothering, and to welcome that as a positive development.

Finally, are you willing largely to miss out on life's most enriching and rewarding experience, an experience that will benefit both you and your child for the rest of your lives? Remember that you will never be able fully to appreciate the many challenges, profound responsibilities, and fantastic freedoms of mainly mothering unless you give it a go.

A young and ambitious friend recently recalled mournfully that she had been in charge of vast sums of money on behalf of the government department for which she had worked until her baby was born. And now, I thought in my aged wisdom, you are in charge of a life.

The works

With doubts about the value of mothering dispelled and a positive attitude towards mothering firmly established, it is time to examine the job itself in greater detail.

Think of a breast. There isn't a more potent symbol of mothering. The dependency of the child, the self-giving of the mother, the physical and emotional development of the child, all are indicated by the breast. Now, let us look at the breast as a symbol of mothering in its different aspects.

The nipple is the centre of the breast. As the central circle of my model of mothering, it represents the spiritual, most intimate aspect of mothering. This is where the mother meets God and draws nourishment and inspiration, faith, love, and hope, to sustain her in her mothering. It is an aspect of mothering that is important from the very beginning, even before the child has been conceived. It matters in your thoughts about having children, it matters in the love you make that gives birth to a child. This aspect of mothering is obscure to all but the mother herself, for no one can delve into another's soul. This aspect of mothering involves the mother and God as well as, possibly, a priest or spiritual advisor, and cannot be delegated.

Next comes the areola, the darker circle of skin surrounding the nipple. It is the second circle of the model of mothering and represents the emotional aspect of mothering. It is the loving of the child which is the being there for the child. And it is the blending of lives that occurs when the mother can be there for her child. This aspect of mothering, though always important, is most prominent during the first few months after the birth when you find that you have to be there – to hold, to touch, to gaze, to listen, to respond. Only a few people are privileged to observe the bond between a mother and her child. And while the father and siblings, other family members as well as close friends can become involved in this aspect of mothering if they can be there for the child, this aspect of mothering is delegated for long periods of time only at great cost to both the mother and her child.

After the areola, we have the fleshy part or bulk of the breast. This is the third circle of the model of mothering and represents the social aspect of mothering. This aspect of mothering is about helping your child to develop into a person, into a social being. It comes to the fore as soon as your child is mobile. This is a more visible aspect of mothering which, moreover, necessarily involves many more persons beside the mother. Interaction with other children as well as adults – playing, sharing, helping, questioning, obeying, observing – enables your child to find a place among them. In addition to the mother and the father and other family members, neighbours and friends as well as professionals such as playgroup staff, teachers, and coaches, play a vital part in this aspect of mothering. A mother cannot possibly socialise a child by herself; she needs a community behind her and around her to communicate values to her child.

Finally, there is the outer rim of the breast which connects the breast to the rest of the body. This is the fourth circle of the model of mothering and represents the practical aspect of mothering which is about mopping the floor. And tidying up. And shopping for food. And cooking dinner. And getting the children ready for school. It is about the many and diverse tasks you face and the decisions you make every day in looking after your children and running a home. And it is about the repercussions of these tasks and decisions beyond the home. Once your child has started school, it can seem at times that mothering is constituted solely of this aspect of mothering: that all you do or can do as a mother is to make sure your child is rested, washed, clothed, and fed – and on time. This is the most visible aspect of mothering and much of it can be delegated to the children themselves as well as to paid help where financially possible. Mothers, however, need to consider the principles behind the routines that make up this aspect of mothering as they link mothering to remote economic, social, and political processes.

Mothering, then, is made up of different aspects but is, like the breast, a whole. While different aspects of mothering shift in and out of focus at different stages in your child's life, none of the aspects of mothering ever loses its importance: your teenager, for example, still needs you to be there for him. All four aspects of mothering, moreover, are essentially interrelated and indivisible. In other words: you have to take care of the lot! Disconnecting the four aspects of mothering in practice radically diminishes the value or goodness of each one. What good, for example, is it to wash, dress, and feed your toddler but otherwise to avoid spending time with her? What good is it to spend time with your toddler but not to wash, dress, and feed her? What good is it to develop your own spirituality and not to teach your child about love of God and neighbour?

What good is it to tell your child about love of God and neighbour and to fail to follow your own teaching? Not much good. The different aspects of mothering form one coherent whole. By neglecting any of the aspects of mothering, you negate the point and purpose of mothering which is to recreate life and love. This realisation can help you to mother.

As symbolised by the breast, the four different aspects of mothering form a series of four concentric circles – one leads to another. This perspective can also be helpful when thinking about mothering as well as in your day-to-day concerns as a mother. Specifically, when you feel frustrated in any of the aspects of mothering, you may want to look for a remedy in the aspect of mothering represented by the next inner circle. You still have to come up with the solution yourself, but at least you are looking in the right place. Say, for example, you find the household over-whelming. For a solution to this problem with the practical aspect of mothering represented by the fourth circle, you might consider making changes in the social aspect of mothering described by the third circle: perhaps you need to put more effort into sharing your values with your children so as to encourage them to take on responsibility for themselves and others. Or else, you find that your children consistently defy your values in their behaviour. This is a problem within the social aspect of mothering represented by the third circle, so it is worthwhile to check your attitudes and actions relevant to the emotional aspect of mothering, indicated by the second circle: are you spending enough time with your children, time in which you can show your children that you love and appreciate them? Perhaps you find yourself unable to show your children that you love and appreciate them, perhaps you are not sure at times that you love and appreciate your children. For help with the emotional aspect of mothering represented by the second circle turn to the spiritual aspect of mothering represented by the innermost circle, turn to your relationship with God. Fundamentally – centrally – your relationship to God sustains the other three aspects of mothering. It enables you to be there for your children, to instruct your children, and to take care of your children. Your relationship to God, in turn, however, needs to express itself in your relationships to your children – in being there, instructing, and caring – to remain meaningful.

Turning inward, towards the centre of mothering, also has another advantage. You not only find solutions to problems closer to the centre, you also find reassurance. While the circles closer to the periphery tend to dominate your daily routine, the circles closer to the centre indicate the source and significance of that routine. While you are cleaning the bathroom, for example, and are wondering whether you wouldn't be better off sitting in an office somewhere, turn towards the centre to regain a sense of the importance of your activities. As you are cleaning the bathroom (fourth circle), you are providing good example and are thereby encouraging respect in your children for others as well as for property (third circle). As you are cleaning the bathroom, moreover, you are there for your children, albeit in the background, and ready to listen (second circle). As you are cleaning the bathroom, finally, you are mindful of the dignity, yea, sanctifying possibilities inherent in manual work (first circle). Clean the bathroom, therefore, and be glad!

NOTES

1 See Catherine Hakim, *Work-Lifestyle Choices in the 21st Century: Preference Theory* (Oxford: Oxford University Press, 2000).
2 Mainstream feminism would also have done well to take on board Adrienne Rich's perspective on the medical manipulation of women's bodies to further econonomic and political interests. Rich acutely notes, for example, that "'overpopulation' is today regarded as a global problem; yet there is far more concern with [...]

limiting births, than with finding new ways to produce and distribute food throughout the globe", Adrienne Rich, *Of Woman Born* (New York, N.Y.: W.W. Norton & Company, 1986) p. 102.

3 Deborah Jackson, *Three in a Bed* (London: Bloomsbury, 1990) p.27.

4 *Daily Telegraph,* 17 June 2000.

5 G.K. Chesterton, *Brave New Family* (San Francisco: Ignatius Press, 1990) p. 110.

6 See, for example, 'Marriage is good for you': *FYC Family Bulletin,* Autumn 1998;
'Was macht die Spanier so froehlich?': *DFV-Familie,* February 2002.

7 For an extended treatment of this argument, see A. Etzioni, *The Spirit of Community,* (New York, N.Y.: Crown Publishers, 1993b).

8 'When "family-friendly" is a skiver's charter': *The Times,* 1 August 2000.

9 The Christian understanding of human dignity and of the value of human life demands that every human being, regardless of present or potential usefulness to society, receive the care they need.

10 *Analysis,* Radio 4, 29 November 2001.

11 'Vorschlaege zum feministischen Umbau der Arbeit', *die tageszeitung,* 26 June 1997.

12 Stein Ringen, *Citizens, Families and Reform* (Oxford: Clarendon Press, 1997).

13 Besides, and I write this realising full well that I may be hung, drawn, and quartered for it, anything that gives couples pause before seeking out the services of a divorce lawyer is a good thing unless, of course, it is an intrinsically bad thing, like abuse. Financial dependence, however, is not an intrinsically bad thing.

14 I am indebted to Leonie Caldecott, the Catholic journalist and writer, for pointing out this symbiosis of significance to me in 1992. I have been thinking about it ever since.

15 Please note the use of the word 'tend'. I am not arguing, in other words, that the public domain is reserved for men and the private domain is reserved for women.

16 *aisles,* architectural term for the passageways on either side of the nave of the church.

17 St Josemaria Escriva cited in Francis Fernandez, *In Conversation with God,* vol. V (London: Scepter, 1992) p. 43.

18 Jutta Burggraf, *Women's liberation and feminism* (Princeton, NJ: Scepter, 1994) p. 27.

19 Pope John Paul II, *Mulieris Dignitatem* p. 19.

20 In fact, I know it now because our children have already begun to improve this world by improving me.

21 Libby Purves draws this distinction between the urgent need for childcare and the economic need for childcare, *The Times,* 14 June 2005.

22 Not all work does, of course. I taught English to primary school children in Germany where we lived for a year and a half, for example, with baby number three tied to my back in a sling.

23 "[...] it is far more difficult for a day care nursery to provide an environment in which a child will develop normal emotions than it is for a mother, or in her absence, a father, grandparent or childminder", Sir Richard Bowlby, quoted in *The Daily Telegraph,* 21 October 2006.

2
believing

Believing is the spiritual aspect of mothering. It is
represented by the central circle of the model of mothering.
Our spiritual centre sustains and guides us in our
mothering and gives us hope.

Physically, emotionally, as well as, in many ways,
intellectually, mothering is probably the toughest job we'll
ever do. In our relationships with our children, the demands
made on us can break us unless we can draw on our faith
for sustenance, guidance, and hope. It is useful, therefore,
to delve the depths of that faith before we start to mother,
and to keep probing and referring to it throughout our
years of mothering.

In this chapter, I consider the relevance to mothering of
the Christian faith in general and of some of the teachings
of the Catholic Church in particular because I believe that
they give access to truth, and because I have found them
helpful. I hope that my comments will stimulate not only
Christians but also readers of other faiths to develop and
draw on their spiritual centre in the tasks of mothering.
My experience has been that by learning to respect and
appreciate one faith, you naturally come to respect and
appreciate other faiths. This is not the case because all
religions are essentially the same – they are not – but
because in learning to respect and appreciate a particular
faith you develop your spiritual dimension. I would be
very glad, moreover, if this book provided an impetus for

readers of the atheistic persuasion (for atheism, too, is a set of beliefs) to re-examine their rejection of their spiritual dimension, a rejection which more often than not is based on conclusions reached in early adolescence.[1] A rejection, moreover, with which they close themselves off from much that matters to humanity.[2]

A novel idea occurred to me a few years ago. I had, ever since they'd first appeared, hacked away at the little foil covers of new toothpaste tubes with the points of scissors or tweezers until I had made an opening large enough to yield a sufficiently thick flow of toothpaste. Throughout this violent procedure, I had felt annoyed at the existence of the foil covers and dissatisfied with the messy results of my efforts to remove them. It took my husband to point out to me the protrusions on the top of toothpaste tube lids specifically designed to perforate the foil covers in the most agreeable manner. The heavens opened and a ray of bright light lit upon my forehead, and I marvelled at what I recognised to be remarkable providence.

Following this experience, I changed my attitude not only to foil covers on toothpaste tubes but also, and more importantly, to instruction leaflets. I had never had time for instruction leaflets before. For one, I was much too clever to need to read them. Surely, I could figure out how to open, use, operate whatever thing by myself, thank you very much. For another, I did not have the time to bother with small print on flimsy paper. I needed whatever thing *now*, not after I had studied several paragraphs of badly written English. So, whatever-things got bashed, bruised, and beaten. More often than not, the whatever-thing of the moment ended up on my husband's desk for his patient and careful attention over the weekend. Ah, yes, pride and haste, forever man's downfall!

Since my epiphany with the toothpaste lid, I *look* for providence. And, lo and behold, I find it. I look at the pictures on the side of juice containers and (generally) manage to open them without spillage. I read the writing on the packaging of some unidentifiable toy our ten-year-old has been given and, voila, manage to make it not only work but even to resemble something familiar, to his delight and my satisfaction. I would go so far as to say that I have found a new humility – and that I am thriving on it. These days, whenever I read "for best results, follow manufacturer's instructions", I nod sagely and gratefully.

Now, my point is not only that I have had, and doubtless still have, a lot to learn but a point of wider significance: that Providence is out there, that we need humility to see it, that finding Providence is joyful, and that following our Maker's instructions is the best way to proceed. I propose, in other words, that theology is good, but that applied theology is better: that the wood of the cross is meant for a rudder, not a picture frame. I suggest, simply put, that we allow our beliefs to inform our attitudes and actions. Perhaps some readers find this suggestion altogether too obvious, but I suspect that for many readers their faith is, as it was for me, rather like the ignored instruction leaflet or, more biblically, like the treasure hidden in the field and quite unlike the coin found. Perhaps, like me, they have been too clever and too busy to look and have yet to discover and put to use the wealth that is theirs. Looking and applying what we find, however – following our Maker's instructions – is profoundly rewarding.

God's authority over us derives from His understanding and love for us.[3] God made us. God therefore knows best what we are capable of and how we can find fulfilment as human beings. God loves us and wants what is best for us. He does not want our self-satisfied and indolent comfort, our easy tolerance of our own and others' failings. No, God wants what is best for us: He wants our perfection, our happiness, our salvation. And there is no other route to perfection, happiness, and salvation than through Him, with Him, and in Him. We cannot do better, therefore, than to hear and obey His Word. To do this, we need to put aside pride and the temptation to rush along with the crowd. But when we do gather up our strength and courage and do that radical, unconventional thing and are Christians in practice, in our attitudes and actions, then we will be blessed.

As with eating food that is healthy or taking physical exercise, we often know what we should be doing but lack the motivation, the will, to do it. So we get stuck in our rut and build up our defences. We maintain that what we did must have been the right thing to do because we did it, and that what we do must be the right thing to do because we are doing it. There is no logic to the arguments but they are certainly the most common and, to many, most convincing justifications for any course of action. We probably imagine that we are asserting our freedom and independence by arguing in this manner whereas we are, in fact, slowly but surely building a cage for ourselves. We invent our personal histories which not only justify and make sense of our past and present attitudes and actions but also ensure that we do not change. And all the while we are unhappy because we are not who we know we should be. Somehow, in some part of us, we realise that sin diminishes us. And we realise that it is only in union with God, our Maker, that we can achieve true greatness and dignity.[4]

> The outer ring of Christianity is a rigid guard of ethical abnegation and professional priests; but inside that inhuman guard you will find the old human life dancing like children, and drinking wine like men; for Christianity is the only frame for pagan freedom. But in the modern philosophy the case is opposite; it is its outer ring that is obviously artistic and emancipated; its despair is within.[5]

Like the personal trainer, for those who can afford one, the Church prods us to do what, in conscience, we know we should do. She helps us to leave our sinful securities behind and begin afresh, to look ahead to glory rather than back at ignominy. She also helps us out of the quagmires of endless intro- or retrospection[6] and helps us instead to focus on the path ahead. We don't pay the Church £40 an hour and are, therefore, perhaps less inclined to take her advice to heart. But she leads the way, anyway, and all we have to do is follow. Sometimes – often – we won't quite understand why we should do what the Church, our personal trainer, instructs us to do. Then we must utter Mary's "yes" and ponder things and trust that understanding will be given us. And we will discover that obedience to God, unlike submission to sin, is always liberating. "When we let ourselves be led whither we will not and where we at first see no meaning, it is then that He leads us out of our own ways and our own thoughts into His thoughts and ways and so into truth, into genuine fullness".[7] And then we will be free.[8]

Beside the image and inspiration of Mary, the Church offers us specific guidelines concerning the context and the practice of mothering. In these guidelines, the Church translates God's wisdom for our use. The guidelines are, as it were, our Maker's instructions. They are not, as is often supposed, designed to impose difficulties on us for the sake of – what? The delight of mischievous Vatican officials? The satisfaction of a spiteful God? No. The guidelines which the Church upholds are reflections of truth. They are about maintaining faith in the possibility of individual and collective change for the better instead of simply and naively approving every prevalent practice and opinion. They are about building the kingdom of God in the face of sin and hopelessness. More specifically, these guidelines are about who we are as human beings. Following these guidelines helps us to live our lives fully and well, to be who we are meant to be – and God knows who we are meant to be. And it is when we are who we are meant to be that we find happiness and fulfilment. "Because He to whom we submit is Love, [our submission] does not impose anything on us from the outside, but liberates us deep within."[9] The chief aim of God's order, after all, is "to give room for good things to run wild"![10]

Husbands and wives

Mothering, the Church teaches, should take place in the context of marriage. Despite appearances to the contrary created by the media, few people who have any idea what mothering involves would, when probed, disagree with this proposition. Given the enormous challenges, complexity, and significance of mothering, who would choose to do it unsupported by a husband? And that, perhaps, is the point. Single motherhood is rarely the option of choice. Single mothers tend to face the enormous challenges, the complexity, and the significance of mothering not only on their own but also, more often than not, preoccupied with hurt or loneliness. Single mothers therefore should receive every possible help and support from their relatives, friends, and wider communities as well as, where possible, financial support from their children's fathers.[11]

The Church offers two guidelines aimed, among other things, at preventing the necessity of mothering alone. Sex, the Church teaches, should be confined to married couples. It is well known that so-called accidents happen, that a child is conceived when the couple making love have no intention of conceiving a child. But 'accidents' really is a misnomer. The conception of a child is not an accident – it is a gift of life. Every time. Given, then, that there is the possibility of this gift from God when a couple make love, it makes sense that the couple should have thought about having children together. It makes sense that the woman should have decided that, yes, she would welcome this man's child; that the man should have decided that, yes, he would welcome this woman's child. It makes sense that both should have committed themselves to the other and decided to build on the stability and the quality of their relationship and to forgo the short-lived pleasures other relationships promise. It makes sense that the couple should enjoy the recognition and the support of their families and friends and of the wider community, including the taxman. And it makes sense that the couple should have placed themselves into God's hands and asked Him to bless their relationship. It makes sense, in other words, that a couple who make love are married. It is a matter of being prepared for life.

The Church's teaching on contraception is an integral part of her teaching on marriage.[12] The Church, alone, it seems, in a wilderness of pseudo liberation, realises that the body is no trivial matter. It is in the Church, therefore, where *our compulsions are recognised and robed as destinies.*[13] Referring to our sexuality, Pope Benedict XVI explains that "what is biological in man is not only biological, but an expression and fulfilment of our humanity".[14] The Church recognises the significance of sex as our participation in the divine creation of life as well as the significance of sex as the intimate and mutual giving of selves. Contraceptives, on the other hand, trivialise sex and thereby promote "the trivialisation of the body, which inevitably includes the trivialisation of man".[15] Contraception encourages us to understand the body solely as an object for pleasure because contraceptives detach sex from its deeper significance. By using contraceptives, we try to cut out the divine element in sex and are commonly also refusing to offer ourselves and to accept the other wholly through the sexual act. As our bodies necessarily involve ourselves, we cannot separate what we do with our bodies in or out of bed from who we are. When we use bodies – ours and others' – as objects, therefore, we are effectively using persons as objects and are thereby diminishing ourselves and others, and sex itself.

Unlike contraceptives, fertility management respects sex by not interfering with its creative potential.[16] Fertility management also respects men and women, created, as they are, as bodies and souls. Fertility management is, moreover, a highly effective method of family planning and recognised as such by the World Health Organisation, although not a quick fix solution, nor a money-spinner for pharmaceutical companies.[17] Instead, fertility management reinforces good practice in marriage as it requires, in addition to the notorious charts and thermometers, *communication* with each other, *consideration* for each other, and *constancy*, that is, faithfulness[18] to each other, as well as a degree of *creativity* during the periods of abstinence. A good thing all round, really.

Confining sex to marriage and including God in the act makes both for better sex and for better habits. Conjugal chastity "humanise[s] our sexual energy"; it makes "sexuality blossom for love".[19] And love, in turn, makes sex profoundly pleasurable and ensures that we do not feel empty or used afterwards. The self-mastery required to confine sexual relations to marriage and the inclusion of God in the spouses' mutual self-giving, moreover, "helps the spouses to become strong in virtue and makes them rich with spiritual goods. [...] It aids spouses in becoming more tender with each other and more attentive to each other. It assists them in dispelling that inordinate self-love that is opposed to true charity."[20] And such good sex and such good habits strengthen marriages.

The Church further teaches that marriage is indissoluble. Jesus' disciples were struck by this one. "If such is the case with husband and wife, it is better not to marry," they grumbled.[21] But, again, God and the Church have decreed what is to our best advantage. Divorce is an extremely stressful process which in most cases leads to further unhappy relationships and loneliness as well as the problems of single parenting. Divorce, moreover, has lasting and devastating effects on the children involved. My own parents and my two siblings and I suffered through divorce. We children missed our father as our father as opposed to an every-other weekend uncle, and we missed our father as a support for our mother. The stress of drawn-out acrimonious divorce proceedings, work, and raising three children on her own took a heavy toll on our mother. Only incredible determination fuelled by inexhaustible hope saw her through it. I vowed I would never repeat my parents' mistakes and then, years later, found myself in a similar sad mess. My husband and I separated, with my husband moving into rented accommodation but returning home at weekends to see the children. I felt tense, and confused, and bitter.

Thank God, my husband and I came through at the other end, feeling incredibly grateful and more content in our marriage than ever. That, according to research, is generally the experience of couples who manage to stay together despite serious difficulties: "eighty-six per cent of people who were unhappily married in the late 1980s, and stayed with the marriage, indicated when interviewed five years later that they were happier. Indeed, three-fifths of the formerly unhappily married couples rated their marriages as either 'very happy' or 'quite happy'".[22] If a marriage survives a crisis, the chances are high that it will improve significantly. The pain, in the end, can be a great gain. Many couples never get to discover this.

Often husbands and wives opt for divorce because they cannot bear to confront their own shortcomings; they have to leave the relationship in order to leave their self-image intact. They are then destined to repeat the same mistakes again and again, in a vicious cycle of failings and recriminations. If confronted, however, marital difficulties are an opportunity to grow as people. Marital difficulties are an opportunity to become more aware of our own needs and to learn to communicate our needs without accusing or prejudging the other. Marital difficulties are an opportunity to realise that focusing on someone else's deficiencies is a waste of time and energy. Marital difficulties are an opportunity to face up to our own character-flaws and to work to overcome them. Marital difficulties are an opportunity to become aware of our lack of wisdom and understanding and to open up to God's guidance though prayer and patience. Marital difficulties are an opportunity to come to appreciate another person's needs and to give of oneself for that person's good. Marital difficulties are an opportunity to appreciate the fact that it is not so much love which makes commitment endure but commitment – faith and discipline – which makes love endure. Given these important opportunities which marital difficulties offer, it would be a pity to escape from them into the, only apparently, easier option of divorce.

It seems to me, then, that there are at least four good reasons for getting married: 1. sex, obviously, 2. companionship and mutual support, certainly, 3. children, hopefully, and 4. perhaps more surprisingly, self-development. The ongoing and intimate confrontation with another person that is marriage challenges us and prompts us to achieve greater maturity. Marriage does this, however, only if the marriage itself provides a stable environment for our growth, if, in other words, the marriage itself is not open to debate.[23] *Your will is wonderful indeed: therefore I obey it. The unfolding of your word gives light and teaches the simple.*

Fortunately, God does not leave it at helpful preaching from the pulpit. He made us and He *mothers* us. He is there, beside us, to guide us through difficulties so that we can indeed come through at the other end, blessed and grateful, wiser for the experience, and content. God can help us in many ways – as long as we let Him. Marriages frequently falter, for example, because the woman's expectations of her husband exceed his capacity. She looks to the man to confirm her value as a human being. But only God can properly do that. "Only God can welcome a person's total surrender in such a way that one does not lose one's soul in the process but wins it".[24] When a wife begins to develop her relationship to God, she becomes free to grow as she feels herself loved and valued. As her orientation shifts away from her husband, in turn, the pressure to fulfil her expectations lifts off him and he, too, becomes free to grow. In restoring her relationship to God, the wife restores herself. And in restoring herself, she helps to restore her relationship to her husband. This, in turn, gives her husband the opportunity to restore himself through his relationship to God. So, if you haven't done so yet, make your twosome a threesome: look up to God, not across to your husband, for confirmation of your self. This allows you both the security and the space to grow. And as genuine growth entails growing towards God, you both will be growing closer together.

During marital turmoil, moreover, we often suffer from conflicting emotions accompanied by the sense that we need to take decisive action. Friends, more likely than not and with the best of intentions, will only tell us what we want to hear, convinced as they are by our perspective and eager to support us. Similarly, marriage counsellors will have us talk our heart out but will generally refrain from telling us that we are wrong to think or behave as we do. When we focus on God during such times, however, and, with help, for example from a priest, attempt obedience to God's word, we make room for new emotions and new possibilities beyond our muddled minds. We give our torn selves a rest, as it were, as we feel ourselves cradled by God. If we manage to practise prayer and patience during difficult times, if we stop listening to our own moans and shouts and try to listen to God instead, we can reach beyond our own sinfulness. "Christ's grace is not superimposed from outside of man's nature, it does not violate it, but liberates and restores it beyond its frontiers."[25] When we remain quiet and receptive, our sinfulness can become transfigured.[26] After a period of prayer and patience we, like the caterpillar after its period of pupation, can emerge from the net in which we had wrapped ourselves with a new strength and a new vision – and fly.

The holy priest who saw me through our marriage crisis told me quite simply to be kind to my husband and to pray for him. That was the best advice I could have received. My inclination had been to grimace and turn my back whenever I saw my husband and to entertain unkind thoughts of him when I didn't. But I attempted obedience and through it not only restored my dignity but also helped to heal our relationship. A fundamental insight of modern psychology is that our actions influence our attitudes; smiling when we do not feel like it can actually make us happier. Use, in other words, affects essence. Gertrud von le Fort once described kindness as the summit of fortitude.[27] Well, I discovered that kindness not only is an expression of fortitude, it also creates fortitude! When we are kind in times of weakness, we actually become stronger. Treating my husband with kindness and keeping him in my prayers while I felt resentment towards him eventually helped to ease my resentment and helped me to see him in a kinder light. The discipline, moreover, allowed me to distance myself from the confused emotions I felt and released me from my fixation on my own position vis-à-vis my husband. It helped me to shift my focus outside of my self, and to surrender my pride and my will to my loving Maker. The docility of my actions led to an inner tranquillity. My inner tranquillity, in turn, rendered me able to receive God's strength and graces, allowing me to change and to grow. I stopped putting myself under pressure (to judge, to decide), admitted my ignorance and help-lessness, and let God do His work. And God did His work. Reconciliation came with a kiss on Christmas Day. And, God knows, it keeps coming.

C.S. Lewis knew that we "do not fail in obedience through lack of love, but have lost love because [we] never attempted obedience".[28] Obedience to the truth is a marvellous discipline. It takes considerable and continuous effort, but it gives light and space and strength and hope. It allows us to be the best we can be, in the most profound sense of that phrase. Our mothering Maker knows best.

Mothers and babies

We have seen, then, how the Church's teachings on sex and marriage benefit us and our children. The Church offers a further guideline which is also intimately linked to our vocation as mothers: the Church teaches that abortion is not a right but a wrong. The Church teaches, in other words, that mothering begins at conception. Any woman who has tried to conceive and then indeed conceived a child knows with her whole being – body, mind, heart, and soul – that the Church's teaching is true: she knows that a little life has been given to her and that she must cherish and nurture that life. Most women who miscarry therefore grieve profoundly for the loss of their child. Their grief frequently goes unacknowledged in our society which habitually denies life to the unborn.[29]

Many women who, for whatever reason, do not welcome the little life they have received nonetheless also feel the truth of the Church's teachings. Whereas they may in the past have considered abortion the obvious course of action in such a situation, once they have actually conceived, many feel torn as to what to do. In fact, ninety-five per cent of women who see ultrasound pictures of their unborn baby or hear their baby's heartbeat do not abort.[30] It appears, then, that a woman can consent to abortion only by denying the reality of what abortion is: when she is confronted with the human life she is carrying, her determination to abort wanes. Of those women who nonetheless opt for abortion, many do so as a result of pressure applied to them by the father of the child[31] or friends or family. And many of the women who have had a termination suffer a severe sense of loss as well as depression for years afterwards.[32] The point of the Church's teaching on abortion is to help us to live our humanity fully, not to deny any aspect of it for the sake of questionable values.

I recently visited a castle in Germany. It was an imposing, largely intact eighteenth-century building set on a high rock, overlooking a picturesque town and, beyond the town, the Elb River and the wooded hills of southern Saxony. And it was empty. I was puzzled – the building and the situation had great potential; if not a hotel chain, the German youth hostel association, surely, would have snapped it up. Then I saw the plaque. During World War II, Nazi doctors put to death some 10,000 mental health patients in this castle. Nobody, I expect, wants to confront those ghosts.

But the ghosts still haunt Germany. The German debate on embryo stem-cell research, for example, returns again and again to the nightmare of medical experiments on human beings under the Nazis, a nightmare which gives pause to contemporary German politicians and scientists. And yet, abortion, as in the UK, is readily available in Germany today. Pregnant women in their thirties or older, for example, are expected to have an amniocentesis carried out to determine the health of their baby. If the baby is found to have an abnormality, the mother can choose to have her baby aborted. I have yet to come across a German who draws the beckoning analogy with the elimination of human beings – Jews, gypsies, communists, the disabled – who did not suit the Nazi lifestyle. A kindergarten teacher I met simply lamented the fact that, due to abortion, there were fewer and fewer children with Down's syndrome attending the integrated kindergarten where she had worked for decades. "They have so much love to give," she said. Most Germans, most Britons, will never know this about children with Down's syndrome. Nazi killers also did not get to know their victims, and dispatched them with similar efficiency.

The Nazi analogy is harsh, I know. Yet the utilitarian denial of the intrinsic value and dignity of human life which the Nazis promoted in their policies and pursued so systematically in their practices also informs contemporary perspectives and practices in Britain. What right do we have to eliminate the human lives – to dismember, stab, poison, suffocate, starve,[33] and bin the babies – who threaten our lifestyle because they are conceived when we feel too young or too old (forty per cent of babies conceived by women over the age of forty are aborted in the UK![34]), when we have slept with the wrong man, when we have other plans? What right do we have to eliminate the human lives – to dismember, stab, poison, suffocate, starve, and bin the babies – who threaten our lifestyle because they are not as we think they should be? We, rightly, feel outraged at the selective abortion practised in India and China, where male children are considered the superior asset to families, and yet we practise similarly motivated selective abortion in this country: the baby that is deemed inferior is killed. Every human being is created in the image of God, not only the ones who suit our lifestyle. The Nazis rejected this truth, we need to retrieve it.

There are two big industries which complement each other perfectly. On the one hand, there is the contraception, pre-natal screening, and abortion industry, whose business it is to prevent, sort, and kill human life. On the other hand, there is the fertility industry, whose business it is to help to create human life against the odds and at the expense of its clients' considerable distress, pain, and money, as well as of shelved and ultimately discarded embryos. Are we possibly duped by the powers behind these industries into promoting and doing what goes quite against our interests? Has casual sex, for instance, tended to increase health and happiness across the population or sexually transmitted infections[35] and heartache? Has the so-called right of women to have abortions tended to enhance their status or has it shot women in the foot by denigrating the dignity and value of human life and therefore the dignity and value of mothering? Has pre-natal screening improved our capacity to cherish and accommodate difference? Has the emergence of the 'right to a child' benefited children?[36]

Throughout the Bible, Jesus reminds us that none of us can point a finger. The sins of others, and the sins of mothers, in particular, must force us to look at ourselves and at the society we have made. "There is much more to being pro-life than being anti-abortion!"[37] Being pro-life means working for a society that values and therefore protects mothers and babies. Being pro-life therefore means fighting against economic and sexual exploitation. Being pro-life means promoting the provision of adequate healthcare throughout the world. Being pro-life also means protecting that which sustains life: our planet. Being pro-life means advocating a profound change in priorities.[38] "Faith in the God of life, who has created every individual as a 'wonder'"[39] is our mainstay in this tremendous task. Such faith helps us to see "in every person His living image" and to "see life in its deeper meaning, [to] grasp its utter gratuitousness, its beauty and its invitation to freedom and responsibility".[40] Being pro-life means celebrating life.

Imagine with me a society in which the factories of death are turned into homes of life. Imagine a society in which *every* conception of a child is treated as the miracle and gift it is. Imagine a society in which the money spent on abortions is instead used to pamper pregnant women in need like princesses: to offer them ready access to shelter, financial support, and counselling so that nobody, nobody, has to consider the killing of their own child their preferred option. Imagine a society in which the money spent on IVF is used instead to facilitate the adoption of some of the babies of those pampered princesses, so that nobody has to consider the extremely costly[41] artificial generation of human embryos their preferred option. Imagine a society in which mothers generally and mothers of children with special needs in particular receive significant assistance from the state and the economy as well as the local community, so that everybody is aware of the importance of mothering. Imagine a society, then, which consistently chooses life over death. The two complementary industries and their associated profiteers would lose out. Everyone else would gain.

I have pointed to the Providence behind the paragraphs of some of our Maker's instructions relevant to mothering. Our Maker's instructions are designed for our benefit and following them is the best possible path to self-fulfilment, a path that has little to do with pursuing narrowly defined self-interest. We can rush along in our pride and haste and with our limited understanding and bash, bruise, and beat what we have been given. Or we can make the best of it – and of ourselves. As the local health club puts it to my delight: "One life. Live it well."

There ought to be a book called *The Joy of God*. It would, more so even than *The Joy of Sex* and *The Joy of Cooking*, be the ultimate how-to Bible: it would help us to live holy lives. It would help us to understand that, while good sex and good cooking certainly are causes of joy, there is no cause of joy like God. It would help us to realise that holiness is the gateway to happiness. It would help us to discover that our Maker's instructions are, if we follow them, the music that turns our doings into dance.

I certainly know, however, how difficult it is to follow instructions! The strength of our ego, the thrust of our socialisation, the force of popular opinion so often get in the way of our pursuit of holiness. Since, as mothers, we have not got the option of retreat into cloistered walls or, better yet, a hermit's cave, we cannot but do battle in the thick of it, and do our best. So it is just as well that our Lord who died on the cross to redeem us has his arms opened wide to embrace us. Christ is merciful and patient. He gives us strength and hope, as we, like children, pick ourselves up after each fall, and begin again.

Grace

There is, of course, more to being Christians in practice than following our Maker's instructions. When we put aside pride and haste and listen to His Word, we discover

59

not only the pathway best suited to us, we also discover that God loves us. In a profound way, our experience of God's love – of his unconditional love and his great mercy and his guiding hand – is the foundation of our relationships with others. I can love because God loves me. I can fail and face my faults and try again – to be kinder, gentler, more patient – because I know that God stands by me despite my failings. I can forgive because I have experienced God's forgiveness. I can persevere when difficulties and sorrow threaten to overwhelm me because I trust in God, I trust that His loving will is good. I can hope because I believe in God's promise. Without love, forgiveness, perseverance, and hope, relationships are impossible. With love, forgiveness, perseverance, and hope, relationships are possible. God teaches us to love, to forgive, to persevere, and to hope.

St John's Gospel relates that Jesus left instructions to "love one another as I have loved you".[42] How has He loved us? This question is worth pursuing for, it turns out, He has loved us like the perfect mother. God mothers us. By mothering us, He equips us, as a mother equips her children, for life: He enables us to share ourselves with others, to fulfil our responsibilities, and to cope with difficulties. Thus enabled, we can face life in general, and mothering in particular. By mothering us, moreover, God gives us an example to emulate: by considering how God mothers us we can learn how to mother. The Christian faith is the best child-rearing guide imaginable. If we live our faith and pass on what we receive, we will be good mothers. It is as simple, and as challenging, as that.

The love with which God loves us and with which we can come to love our children is a love that provides structures and instructs us so that we may become holy and happy. It is a love that shows the loved-one the path of virtue. It is a love that motivates and leads by example, and that helps to overcome failings. The love with which God loves us and with which we can come to love our children is a love that is constant. It is a love that is always there for the loved-one. It is a love that is available, attentive and responsive. The love with which God loves us and with which we can come to love our children is a love that forgives. It is a love that does not judge the loved-one. It is a love that condemns the sin but loves the sinner. It is a love that allows the loved-one to return to the path of virtue. The love with which God loves us and with which we can come to love our children is a love that perseveres. It is a love that can wait patiently for the loved-one to grow in virtue. It is a love that values the loved-one for who the loved-one is, and sees what the loved-one can become. The love with which God loves us and with which we can come to love our children is a love that hopes. It is a love that finds joy in this life and looks forward to even greater joy in the next. It is a love that does not despair. The love with which God loves us and with which we can come to love our children is a love that teaches the loved-one to love.

God has taught me a lot about mothering. Through Mary, God has taught me about the dignity and value of the vocation of mothering. Through the Church, God has taught me about the best context for mothering and the sanctity of life. And through mothering me, God has taught me how to mother: how to love and how to guide our children, how to ask for forgiveness and how to forgive, how to persevere, and how to hope. I have let God imbue my attitudes and actions as a mother, and He has made my experience of mothering rich and rewarding. I have found God in mothering, and mothering in God.

God has taught me a lot about mothering, but there is one lesson which I like best. God has taught me that, with the grace of God, we can live and love with godlike grace. He has taught me that when we listen to His Word and remain close to His love we can be free and simple and open to grace, to those unexpected and undeserved gifts that fill us with joy and gratitude.

The day after my husband and I got back from our

honeymoon, we dived into the pile of wedding presents and discovered a little cherub. Not a real one. It was hand-carved from wood and painted. None of our guests had given it to us, as far as we could tell. The cherub has since graced what became the baby room. It symbolises for us the occasions when we are surprised by joy; it represents God's unsought for blessings. It represents grace.

Grace is a gift given out of an abundance of love. The love with which God loves us and with which we can come to love our children is a grace-bestowing love. It is a love that blesses the loved-one. Being open to grace helps wives and mothers to be gracious; it helps us to pass on our blessings. Grace is Christmas which brings warmth and light where it was cold and dark. Grace is Easter Sunday which celebrates hope and life when all was despair and death. Grace is my husband's smile after an exhausting day. Grace is the mother dropping the duster to take her squabbling children for a walk in the sun.

It is then, when we feel touched by grace, that we know with the certainty of children how wonderful it is to have a Father in Heaven who knows how to mother us.

NOTES

1 For a literary example of this common uncritical adherence to adolescent convictions relating to matters of faith, see the Uber-middleclass protagonist in Ian McEwan's novel *Saturday*.

2 "A reason which is deaf to the divine and which relegates religion into the realm of subcultures is incapable of entering into the dialogue of cultures. [...] listening to the great experiences and insights of the religious traditions of humanity, and those of the Christian faith in particular, is a *source of knowledge*, and to ignore it would be an unacceptable restriction of our listening and responding," Pope Benedict XVI, 'Three Stages in the Program of De-Hellenization', address delivered to scientists at the University of Regensburg, 12 September 2006 (my italics).

3 The Lithuanian psychiatrist Gintautas Vaitoska, M.D. notes in his excellent article on contraception, 'For men of our time...' (*Linacre Quarterly Review*, November 1994), that liberal thought suspects any authority because it assumes that authority is necessarily about the exercise of power over others.

4 Cf. *Mulieris Dignitatem*, 9. This is a central point of John Paul II's 'Apostolic Letter on the Dignity and Vocation of Women', as of much of his teaching.

5 G.K. Chesterton, *Orthodoxy* (London: Hodder & Stoughton, 1996) p.235.

6 C.S. Lewis in *The Pilgrim's Regress* presents a graphic image for this peculiarly modern preoccupation: men and women who spend their entire time staring at their own and others' upset and upsetting insides.

7 Cardinal Joseph Ratzinger [*Co-Workers of the Truth*, p.18] Homily, Cathedral of Our Lady, Munich, July 7, 1984.

8 "To penetrate into Jesus' sentiments means not to consider power, wealth and prestige as the highest values in life, as in the end, they do not respond to the deepest thirst of our spirit, but to open our heart to the other, to bear with the other the burden of life and to open ourselves to the Heavenly Father with a sense of obedience and trust, knowing, precisely, that if we are obedient to the Father, we will be free," Pope Benedict XVI, June 1, 2005, address at general audience, Vatican City.

9 Pope Benedict XVI, address delivered from a ship on the Rhine River to young people gathered in Cologne, 18 August, 2005 for World Youth Day.

10 Ibid: 138.

11 I refrain from advocating government support for single mothers *which exceeds that for married couples* because governments taking such a role, as the British 'experiment' has shown, can promote the choice of single motherhood-as-career among young women and encourage irresponsibility among fathers, cf. Patricia Morgan, *Farewell to the Family?* (London: The IEA Health and Welfare Unit, 1999).

12 Cf. *Humanae Vitae*.

13 Cf. Philip Larkin's poem 'Church Going'.

14 Pope Benedict XVI, 'The anthropological foundation of the family (part 1)', address to the Congress of the Diocese of Rome, June 9, 2005.

15 Ibid.

16 For more information on fertility management, contact one or several of the following: info@lifefertility.co.uk; bomtrust@btconnect.com;

info@fertilitycare.org.uk; enq@naomi.ie; mark@zoes-place.org; info@naprofertility.co.uk; www.cclgb.org.uk

17 Funding from pharmaceutical companies for the educational activities of Brook Advisory Centres in the UK amounted to £66,559 over the period 1993-1999, *FYC Family Bulletin*, Winter 1999/2000. Pharmaceutical companies obviously know how to boost business!

18 Faithfulness in marriage is, incidentally, the best way to avoid catching sexually transmitted infections, most of which can spread despite condom use. The World Health Organisation, no less, therefore recommends staying faithful for life to one person whom you know is uninfected, see 'Sexual spin: sorting fact from fiction about sexually transmitted infection' (Twickenham: The Family Education Trust).

19 Gintautas Vaitoska, M.D. 'For men of our time...', *Linacre Quarterly Review*, November 1994.

20 *Humanae Vitae*, 21.

21 Matthew 19:3–10.

22 Unpublished research by Linda J. Waite, cited in FYC Family Bulletin, Issue 105, Autumn 2001, and in Linda J. Waite and Maggie Gallagher, *The Case for Marriage* (New York: Doubleday, 2000) p. 148.

23 The sociologist Anthony Giddens makes a similar point. In his book *Modernity and Self-Identity* (Cambridge: Polity Press, 1991) he has this to say about so-called 'pure relationships', relationships, that is, which lack an external referent:
"Pure relationships are double-edged. They offer the opportunity for the development of trust based on voluntary commitments and an intensified intimacy. [...] The pure relationship [therefore] is a key environment for building the reflexive project of the self, since it both allows for and demands organised and continuous self-understanding – the means of securing a durable tie to the other. [...] *But shorn of external moral criteria*, the pure relationship is vulnerable as a source of security at fateful moments and at other major life transitions. Moreover, the pure relationship contains internal tensions and even contradictions. By definition, it is a social relation which can be terminated at will, and is only sustained in so far as it generates sufficient psychic returns for each individual. [...] The possibility of dissolution, perhaps willingly brought about by the individual in question, forms part of the very horizon of commitment. It is not surprising that rage, anger and depressive feelings swirl through the contexts of pure relationships and, in concrete circumstances, intimacy may be psychically more troubling than rewarding" (p. 187, my italics).

24 Edith Stein, *Woman*, trans. Freda May Oben (Washington: Institute of Carmelite Studies, 1987) p. 62.

25 Benedict XVI, 'The anthropological foundation of the family (part 2)', address to the Congress of the Diocese of Rome, June 10, 2005

26 Cf. Fr David McGough: *The Catholic Herald*, 9 March 2001.

27 cited in Francis Fernandez, *In Conversation with God*, vol. 1(London: Scepter, 1994) p. 340.

28 C.S. Lewis, *That Hideous Strength* (New York: Simon & Schuster, 1996) p. 147.
An atheistic friend recommended C.S. Lewis' science fiction trilogy to me, of which this is the third volume. I am not sure what she sees in it, I must ask her. I see in it the breadth and depth and beauty of Christianity, and cannot recommend the books highly enough.

29 "Women say again and again that people don't understand the depth of their loss. They understand that it's an unhappy occasion but they expect the sadness to be a fleeting thing. Because there is nothing to be seen, they cannot relate to it as a child, but for the woman, the baby is a person from the word 'go'," Ruth Bender Atik, national director of the *Miscarriage Association* quoted in *ladies first*, winter 1996/97. For further information, contact the *Miscarriage Association*, c/o Clayton Hospital, Northgate, Wakefield, West Yorkshire, WF1 3JS. Also see books such as Anne Oakley, *Miscarriage* (Penguin); Ingrid Cohn Moffit, *Pregnancy Loss: A Silent Sorrow* (Headway); Christine Moulder, *Miscarriage: Womens' Experiences & Needs* (Pandora Press).

30 Peter Garrett, 'The spirit active and present in life', talk given at The Gift of Hope Symposium, Catholic Chaplaincy, Oxford, 7 March 1998.

31 According to family therapist Helm Stierlin, marriages generally do not survive if a woman had an abortion as a result of pressure from her husband, *Der Spiegel*, 17 February 1992.

32 A study carried out by Dr David Reardon and the Elliot Institute of Illinois, published in the Medical Science Monitor, looked at a national survey of nearly 1,900 women who first became pregnant between 1980 and 1992. Some had abortions, and some gave birth. Those having abortions were 65% more likely to suffer from clinical depression, *Pro-Life Times*, July 2003. Matthew O'Gorman of the organisation *Life* notes that some women do not experience depression brought on by abortion until decades after the event, *The Guardian*, 28 October 2005.
If you need help after an abortion or know somebody who does, you may want to contact *British Victims of Abortion*, www.bvafoundation.org. Their helpline is tel. 0845 603 8501

(open 7 p.m. to 10 p.m., 7 evenings per week, calls charged at local rate).

33 These are procedures employed in the UK to kill the foetus during an abortion.

   Tina Beattie, senior lecturer in Christian Studies at Roehampton University, suspects that if the practice of injecting potassium chloride into the heart was regularly carried out on laboratory rats instead of 22-week-old foetuses, it would cause far greater public outcry, *The Tablet*, 19 March 2005. I fear she is right.

34 Office for National Statistics, *Health Statistics Quarterly*, Spring 1999.

35 Contrary to popular opinion, condoms are only 85-95 per cent effective in preventing HIV transmission and much less effective in protecting from other sexually transmitted infections, in particular common ones such as herpes and HPV, which are spread by skin-to-skin contact with parts not covered by the condom, 'Sexual spin: sorting fact from fiction about sexually transmitted infection' (Twickenham: The Family Education Trust).

36 "Where does this trail of 'rights' end? First the right to have a child, and then the right to have a healthy child, followed by the right to have a child with all the traits of one's choosing. In other words, the right to have a perfect child. These are the commandments of the reproductive industry. [...] Our collective responsibility for children has been replaced by the need to fulfil the individual desires of adults," Aminatta Forna, *The Mother of all Myths* (London: HarperColllins, 1999) p. 154.

37 Tina Beattie, *The Tablet*, 19 March 2005.

38 For more information on pro-life activities, see the website of the *Society for the Protection of Unborn Children*, www.spuc.org.uk., and www.lifecharity.org.uk.

39 *Evangelium Vitae*, 83, cf. also Psalm 139:14.

40 Ibid.

41 Due to the common practice of replacing two embryos in the womb, the numbers of twin pregnancies and twin births have soared in the UK along with their associated risks for the mothers and babies involved, for instance. According to Professor Peter Braude, a fertility specialist at St Thomas's Hospital, the chance of complications in the mother of twins increased sixfold and the risk of death of the babies in the first month of life outside the womb increased sevenfold, *The Independent*, 19 October 2006.

42 John 13:34.

3
loving

Loving is the emotional aspect of mothering. It is represented by the second circle of the model of mothering. The bond between us and our children and the self-giving which characterises that bond is supported by our relationship to God.

Seven days after our first child was born, I ran away. I had not slept for more than a couple of hours at a time for the past week and had had the baby at the breast for the rest of the time except once when I had, guiltily, abandoned our lightly sleeping daughter on our bed for five minutes to have a shower, during which she promptly slipped off the bed and cried whereupon I, stark naked, rushed to her, clutched her to my bosom, sobbed, and worried about brain damage (hers, not mine). It was a Thursday, my husband came home from work and I handed him the baby and left. Though my head felt as though it would fall off from tiredness, my body was raring to get out and stride out in the brisk Spring air. I walked and walked. I walked through the streets and along the river and across the meadow. I barely noticed the trees and the birds but was glad to be on my own and moving fast. After about two hours, I returned home and took our crying daughter and fed her. My husband had held her throughout the time I was gone, unable to console her, wondering whether I would come back.

This was 1993, and my husband and I were incredibly educated and incredibly ignorant. We held five and a half university degrees between us and knew nothing about the reality of caring for a baby. Sure, among friends and in books we had come across the occasional nodding acknowledgement of the challenges ahead of us. Apart from the technicalities involved, however, the physical and emotional details of introducing new life into this world were as taboo at the time as the details of death. Like death, new life was something one was expected to cope with when it happened, as it happened, within one's own four walls, and without previous relevant experience, without even the concepts to put to what was happening. As a result, my husband and I had laboured under the illusion that mothering would come to me as easily as the wish for a baby and, indeed, the baby herself had come to me. We had thought that I would be able to look after our baby on my own, that I would not go insane with tiredness, and that I would readily adjust to the change in my circumstances. We had utterly failed to realise how radically those circumstances would change.

My husband and I were not only ignorant, we were isolated, as well. Though the midwife and then the health visitor came round for inspections and my sister dropped in on her way back from Africa to marvel at the change in me and friends and neighbours visited and admired the baby, nobody stayed and helped. There was no stream of relatives and friends at the door bringing dinners, asking for shopping lists, and volunteering to do the cleaning; no provision at my husband's place of work for cover for him so that he could take some time off; no ready-made network of experienced mothers waiting to catch me and show me the ropes.

So, my husband and I had to grapple on our own with a completely perplexing situation, recognise our needs, and discover ways to meet them. Things got better after that first terribly difficult week. In my own proud and impetuous way, I had taken the first step: I had asked for help. We bought a bottle and my husband took over the night feeds at weekends for a while to help me to catch up on sleep. My mother-in-law came to help out for a couple of weeks and then a Spanish girl moved in for a few months and played with and cuddled our daughter, did some cleaning and the washing up, and pined away for her boyfriend in Malaga. We ordered our first-ever case of red wine for *daily* consumption (the idea was in part that the alcohol in my breast-milk would help the baby to sleep[1]) and, for weeks on end, ate either beans on rice or cauliflower and cheese and potatoes for dinner. Breastfeeding stopped hurting after the first five weeks, and when I no longer required a particular chair in a particular room, five cushions, and total silence for feeding, I quickly learned to feed while reading, eating, talking, and going to the toilet, and came to enjoy the freedom of feeding our daughter outside sitting cross-legged in the grass. I put the baby in the sling and moved about with her in the brisk Spring air. I tore out the first few pages I had written in our daughter's diary, and started again.

Looking back, I see how unnecessary our ignorance and initial isolation were. I can see how much easier the beginning of mothering could be and should be. It is very unfortunate – tragic even – that we get so little social or cultural help with major life changes these days. We are, for example, desperately lacking in rituals that help to guide us from one stage of life to another, so-called rites of passage which help us to become aware of as well as come to grips with new responsibilities. We also lack signs or symbols that mark us out as people who, during our period of transition, need to be treated differently so that we can drop the pretence that nothing extraordinary is happening and that everything is fine, thank you very much. We are, furthermore, lacking in customs that help the people on the sidelines of transition to find an appropriate place for themselves between the extremes of looking on and taking charge, in particular when the transitions concerned involve life or death and the need for help is therefore great.

Given this social and cultural dearth in general and the lack of rites of passage for new mothers in particular, the trauma of giving birth and the shock of motherhood can actually be quite helpful. The near-death experience of the second stage of labour and the otherworldly exhaustion that comes with caring for a newborn are like windows to the sacred in which we, as life-giving mothers, must come to play our part. The trauma and the exhaustion allow us a glimpse, if we manage to look, of vast significance beyond daily cares and hang-ups. They are, furthermore, the elbow in the ribs, the strident call: "pay attention, *all* of you, body, mind, heart, spirit! Things are about to change. *You* are about to change!" It is for this reason that, with hindsight, I can manage to feel grateful for that awful initiation into the process that turned me into a mother. That first week in our daughter's life certainly had the intensity of a rite of passage for me. I was not stripped naked in a shaman's hut to spend a week sweating with my demons, but our firstborn succeeded in keeping me in my pyjamas and confining me to the house while confronting me with my inadequacies. The tremendous physical and emotional strain I experienced put me into a state of "constructive fragility"[2]; it dismantled my self and rendered me malleable, ready to be reconfigured into a self of which my child, my children, would forever constitute a part. The woman who ran away after that first week made her last bid for self-contained individuality. She still rears her head occasionally in fantasies of solitary life on a mountain-top. But the woman who returned was ready to learn to love in a completely new way: to love unconditionally.

Being there

I. In addition to the impromptu rite of passage which initiated me into motherhood there is another, rather more significance-laden, rite of passage which has also helped me with mothering. It was not at all impromptu, in fact, it was planned from the beginning of time, and it is deservedly the best known rite of passage ever undergone by anybody. It is, of course, Christ's death on the cross and his Resurrection. Jesus Christ accomplished rather more in his rite of passage than I accomplished in mine. Through his death and subsequent Resurrection, Jesus revealed to us that he is God. Through his death and Resurrection, moreover, Jesus redeemed mankind. Through his death and Resurrection, furthermore, Jesus transformed suffering. All this is quite enough to ponder, but there is more: since God **is** love and the Redemption was accomplished **for** love of us and **love** alone can transform suffering, the protagonist and the motivation as well as the message of this rite of passage is love. And that makes Christ's ultimate rite of passage relevant to mothers and mothering in several profound ways.

God is love. And God, we know, created man in His own image. This must mean, then, that man is destined to love, that love is man's path as well as his goal. "Man, who is the only creature on earth God willed for itself, cannot fully find himself except through a sincere gift of himself"[3], a gift of self given out of love and for love to another. Nothing makes us more God-like than loving another. "Love is 'divine' because it comes from God and unites us to God".[4] "[Man] becomes like God in the measure that he becomes someone who loves".[5] And of all loves, that love central to mothering, unconditional love – the love that loves no matter what – is most like God's love for us. In allowing our selves to become changed in the course of mothering so as to become capable of unconditional love and in loving unconditionally, we respond to God's call to true self-fulfilment, we respond to God's call to holiness. In thus dying to our old selves and rising again, so to speak, as mothers, we become more fully human and in becoming more fully human we become a little more like God.

God loves us. How much does He love us? He died for us – good enough? Yes, but. How are we to know that He loves us now? Now, when we can't do anything right? Now, when we feel angry, aggressive even? Now, when we are worried and close to despair? It is one thing to believe in God's love, another to enjoy it! Well, we cannot enjoy what we do not know and getting to know something takes time and effort. Coming to know God's love for us requires practising our faith. It requires recalling several times daily God's word, God's will, God's wisdom as we go about our activities, feel our feelings, and think our thoughts. Prayers, both traditional prayers and our own, readings, especially the writings of the many saints – there is bound to be one who speaks to you! – and the Sacraments of Communion and Confession are particularly important aids in this quest. They help us to acknowledge our weakness and entrust it to God, and in entrusting our weakness to God, we approach God's love.

The effort to get to know God's love for us is infinitely worth it. God loves us as His children, unconditionally. He does not love us because we are good and strong. He loves us because we are His children. And His love is what makes us good and strong. God's love for us is "an effective and operative love. [It] is a love which, far from presupposing in us any lovableness, actually produces that lovableness within us".[6] Knowing God's love for us makes us lovable. Our relationship to God, the love at our spiritual core, shapes and sustains our self. Our relationship to God therefore prepares us for mothering, for in mothering, we have to give our self, no less. If we keep turning to God, we can keep turning to our children and love them into health and happiness and holiness.

During my atheistic student days, a strikingly calm and content American friend once remarked over a cream tea that she knew that God loved her. My initial reaction was to try and brush the remark mentally aside ("what an American thing to say!"). But the remark lingered and, eventually, helped to rekindle a desire which in turn prompted a search and a struggle. That search and struggle continue, but I am now far enough along to be able to say, with almost American self-assurance, that God loves me. I have experienced His love in many ways over many years. My calmness and my confidence, and my ability to love others as He loves me, are growing. *I saw how the Lord carried me as if I were a child.*[7]

Love transforms suffering. The sores of our past, the conflicts between us and our own mothers, the chain stretching back perhaps over many generations of more or less abusive mothering – are we destined to pass on all that? Can we give more than we have been given? No, but we have been given so much more than we perhaps realise. We do not have to become our mothers and grandmothers; we do not have to end up sounding like them, suffering like them. We do not have to love with a cold, critical, overbearing, or unpredictable love, even if that was how we have been loved because we now know a different kind of love. We can transcend past patterns because we now know ourselves loved with a perfect love. When we experience God's love for us, we can put our pain behind us. We no longer have need to look back in anger or forward in fear; we can look around in love. Secure in God's creative love, we can pass it on through our love of our children.

> Certainly, as the Lord tells us, one can become a source from which rivers of living water flow (cf. John 7:37-38). Yet to become such a source, one must constantly drink anew from the original source, which is Jesus Christ, from whose pierced heart flows the love of God (cf. John 19:34).[8]

Experiencing God's love for us enables us to reach beyond our past and beyond ourselves to love others with a similarly powerful, transforming love.

73

II. So, what does this wonderful transformative love involve? I mean, are we meant to be *doing* anything here? How is unconditional love communicated?

God's love for us is not only the foundation and fount of our love for our children, it is also the model of the love needed in mothering. And the foremost way in which God expresses His love for us is in being there. God knows us, God listens to us, God responds to us. God gives us His full attention at each and every moment. This is certainly a tough act to follow. Fortunately, we do not have to match His mindfulness. But we have to be there for our children, we have to be available, attentive, and responsive, in particular at the beginning of our children's lives.

There is a great fear of prescriptiveness in writing about baby care, and for good reason, as circumstances and personalities vary greatly. Most writers therefore pay obeisance to that omnipresent contemporary deity, the god of individual choice, and so will I, except on this point. You must be there for your baby. I do not mind how precisely you go about it, though I have plenty of ideas about that as you will see, but you must be there. If you deny yourself and your child the beginning, you deny yourselves more than you will ever know, because afterwards it is too late to find out. At the beginning more than at any other point, you and your child need to communicate much of importance to each other. The beginning is therefore absolutely crucial for both mother and child: it is when mothers are made, the mother-child bond is forged, and the foundation of a new life, your child's life, is laid. Be there.

Since as mothers we are not (quite) God, we need help in order to be able to be there for our baby. It is at this early stage when the husband and father comes into his own in that proverbial supporting role and when relatives and friends as well as employers and society at large need to rally round. In fact, this is one really useful thing the government could do: ensure that *every* mother can be there for her baby. It is a widespread misconception that the mother-baby relationship develops in a bubble and is no one else's responsibility. The mother-baby relationship, however, necessarily develops in a specific social, economic, political, cultural, and religious context and is everybody's responsibility. And it is in everybody's interest to take that responsibility seriously.

And, what do we do in being there? We hold. We touch. We watch. We smile. We listen. We talk. We sing. The routine can wait, must wait for some days or weeks. In the beginning, you and your baby are getting to know each other and that is best done in your baby's own good time. The beginning, moreover, is a period of transition during which you are feeling your way into mothering and your baby is feeling his way into this life and this world. Give yourselves time. Take time. Your life and your child's life necessarily blend at this stage. Don't fight it by imposing a schedule, asserting your independence, taking up sky diving. This is not the time to prove anything. This is the time to be there. Enjoy it! If you can be there for your baby, you will know when you and your baby are ready to move on to establish some rhythm.

Hold your baby as much as you can at the beginning, stroke and cuddle, cradle and nuzzle. If you or your baby feel unsure, fragile, or fractious, baby massage can be a good way to begin at the beginning. There are plenty of books and tapes and even courses teaching baby massage, but the basic moves are simple. Lie your naked baby on a thick towel in a warm and draught-free room, rub some almond oil into your hands and gently stroke your baby's body while maintaining eye contact. You could add it as a little ritual after each nappy change. Baby massage helps both yourself and your baby to become aware of her body as well as to appreciate the warmth and comfort of your touch. You will also both gain trust in, quite literally, your ability to handle your baby.

Another good way to start, in fact 'the best start for your

baby' (as we are so frequently told), is breastfeeding. There is a lot to be said in favour of breastfeeding[9], above all the unrivalled nutritional benefits of your breastmilk[10] as it adapts to your baby's needs and the numerous health benefits to the mother. Breastfeeding is also, once you get the hang of it, incredibly efficient and convenient. Breastmilk, moreover, is very cheap (even if you find, as I did with our first child, that you need an extra meal in 24 hours) and comes in the world's most beautiful environmentally-friendly packaging. And there is one more point in its favour: breastfeeding obliges you to be there for your baby. Given that your breast is attached to your body, you will have to be there with your baby if you are breastfeeding. And that is as it should be in the beginning.

Another excellent and time-proven way of being there is to carry your baby in a sling. Babies have been carried in slings on their mothers' backs for most of human history and are still carried like that in most parts of the globe. There are many significant advantages to carrying your baby. Babies need close physical contact especially in the first few months after birth. Carrying your baby close to your body in a sling reduces the shock of the transition from the womb and gives your baby a sense of security as he feels your familiar warmth and smells your familiar smell and moves with your familiar movements and hears your familiar voice. In addition, evidence suggests that babies who are carried gain weight more quickly. Carrying your baby in a sling, moreover, ensures that your baby is significantly further away from car exhaust than he would be in a pram or push chair, which is a point of concern if you live in a city. Carrying your baby in a sling, finally, and perhaps most importantly, leaves you with your hands unencumbered and your movements unobstructed, which makes being there a lot of the time a lot more feasible – especially if you have a toddler as well as a baby around. Doctors agree that carrying your baby in a sling does not harm your baby's spine as long as the sling supports the spine, and if you carry your baby on your back rather than on your front as soon as possible, you will not harm your own spine either.

I could not have managed mothering without a sling, though I did manage (all four babies) without a pram. The sling we used[11] with each of our children until well into toddlerhood allowed us to carry our babies on the front from birth and on the back from about three months. Oh, the freedom in that! I could do whatever I liked, really, (except go swimming) *and* have my baby close to me at the same time. I did, for example, regularly take our youngest to the park to go 'power walking'. As she grew heavier, I grew stronger. I got my exercise and she got her tour of the local dog population. I only stopped taking her when she started wriggling about too much – with excitement at the dogs – at about eighteen months. I also played with and cuddled an older sibling, cooked and washed-up, went shopping (in and out of buses, through pushy crowds, in and out of shops, up and down stairs...), attended Mass, typed away at my computer, taught English, visited art galleries, negotiated airports, and what-not with a baby on my back. Initially, our babies almost always fell asleep in the sling after a little while, especially if I was moving. As they grew older, they more and more often used their time in the sling to look at the world from their safe vantagepoint.

A further easy and time-proven way of being there is to keep your baby in bed with you at night. Your baby enjoys your close physical presence and you do not have to get up to feed her. It took me a while to catch on to this one with our first baby, but eventually I asked myself what I was doing sitting cold and impatient and uncomfortable in a chair in the middle of the night when I could be feeding our baby while lying comfortably in my warm bed. I never looked back. Sometimes I put the babies back into their cot after a feed, sometimes I kept them with me, depending on how tired I was and what sort of sleepers they were. I so much enjoyed cuddling our babies in bed either on my chest or by my side that I missed them terribly when they outgrew their need for me during the night! Sleeping with your baby in your bed does not present any danger to your baby as long as neither you nor your husband are drunk, drugged, excessively tired, or a smoker and as long as you are, moreover, used to being there for your baby – used to being available and attentive and responsive. Being there is a habit that becomes second nature and that will see your baby safely through the night in your bed even when you are asleep. Keeping your baby in bed with you is, incidentally, also a great way to ensure that you get a mid-day nap if you need one.

Being there further involves, of course, playing with your baby. Babies are incredibly clever and focused, something which anyone who has ever been with a baby (in the sense of being there: available, attentive, and responsive) has known all along but which scientists are now increasingly discovering as well. And playing with your baby stimulates all that innate cleverness. Playing with your baby requires, ideally, anyway, your full attention as you sing or talk to your baby and respond to his responses, as you jiggle or tickle your baby and see how he likes it, as you play peek-a-boo and delight in his surprise, as you shake a rattle and watch whether he follows its noise, as you read to your baby and teach him the sounds cows, ducks and sheep make, and as you do one or another of the silly yet significant things you do with babies to help to provide their focused little minds with food for thought. In all of this, it is important not to overdo it. Babies generally do not need great variety, nor do they require constant stimulation. Babies like repetition and, sometimes, they just want some peace. Play can only help your baby to develop if it is tailored to your baby's temperament and capacity to learn, which is another reason why remaining not only available but also attentive and responsive to your baby is crucial.

It is the playing-with-your-baby aspect of being there

which has always presented me with a particular challenge as I am a mad multitasker; I am forever looking to do something else while I am doing something else.[12] And that is a terrible nuisance of a habit as far as our children are concerned ("look at me, look at me, mum!" says our three-year-old) and not the thing to do when you are playing with your baby. However, if you are like me, do not worry too much about it. Try integrating games into tasks. Peek-a-boo, for instance, is an obvious one to play while dressing your baby. Singing to your baby is also ideal for mad multitaskers as you can sing songs to accompany other activities; we ended up with a song for going to bed, another for cleaning teeth, a song for riding on the bike (from about six months), a song for changing the nappy, a song celebrating the contents of the nappy, etc. And as long as you have your baby around in the sling, on a rug, or in a play pen[13] as you do whatever you are doing, your baby will get plenty of stimulation, especially if you provide a running commentary and pause occasionally to look at your baby and ask your baby a question.

And then, thank goodness, there are ways of being there without quite being there, because sometimes you can't and sometimes you won't. It is a good idea, for example, to swaddle small babies. Swaddling helps to let babies feel held and secure. It also keeps their little limbs from flailing. My husband excelled at swaddling; my packages usually came quickly undone. If you do it right, you have a compact little bundle who, with any luck, will sleep peacefully for a while. When your baby gets older, you can leave her arms unswaddled or put her into a sleeping bag made for babies. We also used a fleece in the cot for our babies, albeit under a cotton sheet (to catch the dribbles etc.). The idea of the fleece is that it simulates the animal warmth and softness of another creature nearby, so using a fleece is another way of almost being there. And, yes, finally, there are the others: the father, above all, but also the siblings, perhaps, and the grandparents, the aunts and uncles, the friends and neighbours. Just think: while you may well be weary from being there more or less continuously, for them a spell at being there is a treat! Let them come, therefore – and pass the baby.[14]

Getting there

I. Love gives time and love takes time. The transformations wrought in the mother by being there do not happen overnight. At first, indeed, being there for your baby may seem to you as though you had been parachuted into a foreign country. Your familiar reference points – your job, your friends, your looks, your brain – suddenly seem remote. As a result of being ill prepared and needlessly isolated as well as of the many demands made on you by your baby, you feel disoriented and inclined to panic. Don't panic.

You may well be suffering from culture shock. Culture shock occurs when you confront the culturally other on an existential level. Becoming a mother involves just that: you are forced to come to terms with an entirely new set of circumstances and its associated body of knowledge – and your baby's life depends on it. You do not know how to accomplish the most basic tasks nor do you know the local lore and the relevant values in this strange place called motherhood. Culture shock shakes you from your securities and forces you to re-examine yourself. As a new mother you are, then, not only exhausted from lack of sleep and overwhelmed by new responsibilities, you are also staring in the face of that eternal question: who am I? It is therefore very understandable that your first instinct may be to try to escape and return to a familiar base. As a mother, however, retreat is not possible.[15] The anthropologist can leave the village in the jungle to write her learned tract for colleagues back home. The mother of a baby, however, is stuck: the other is with her, dependent on her. But there is a cure for culture shock: immersion – getting to know the other as thoroughly as that which you have left behind. Being there, in other words.

Through being there, by taking time and giving time and being open to the other who is your little one and the changes your little one brings, the unfamiliar culture will become known to you and you will become an adept speaker of the native language, as it were. And in this process, your own baby is your best guide. Just as you can study the grammar of a foreign language from books but need to engage with native speakers to appreciate its nuances, books on baby care and advice from friends can prepare you and give you useful general ideas but your baby will show you what precisely works best for your baby – as long as you are available, attentive, and responsive. There is no short-cut to getting to know your baby, there is no short-cut to being there. The anthropologist will have read books about the people in the jungle before getting there, and that was a good thing, too. But once she got there, she put the books away because they got in the way of being there. Similarly, being there, not books, is what makes you a competent mother of your baby.

Through being there, moreover, you will begin to enjoy this totally other culture. It is not what you are used to, it is probably not what you were brought up to value and appreciate, in fact, you may have to overcome a few negative prejudices before you *can* value and appreciate it, but, by and by, you will value and appreciate it. By taking time and giving time, by being available, attentive, and responsive to your baby, you come to understand and to love your baby. And this is the wonderful thing about being there. It is at once what you *should* be doing as the mother of a baby as well as precisely what best helps you to *enjoy* being the mother of a baby. The development of the baby and the mother's enjoyment of her baby are thus tightly intertwined. I think of it as 'the lovely loop': by being there for your baby you gain competence and confidence in your skills as a mother and get to know and love your baby, all of which, in turn, render being there for your baby increasingly enjoyable. Through doing what love requires of you, in other words, you come to enjoy the gifts of love which, in turn, help you to meet the demands of love. When you see a mother gazing lovingly at her baby as though the rest of the world did not exist, you can be sure that they are both caught up in the lovely loop. And there you have it: a slice of Heaven, as defined by Samuel Johnson, at any rate, who suggested in *Rasselas* that "the happiness of heaven will be that pleasure and virtue will be perfectly consistent."

Finally, it helps to realise that this is not the rest of your life. There will come a time to pick up some or all of the threads of your old life, a time when your mind will once again engage in familiar ways. A misleading aspect of the working mothers debate is that it tends to present the issue as a decision between two polar alternatives: either you work outside the home or you stay at home and look after your children. Apart from neglecting the majority of mothers who work part-time or from home, this representation of the issue completely ignores a key dimension: time. Your children's needs as well as your own response to motherhood will vary over time and it does not make sense, therefore, to decide once and for all what sort of a mother you are going to be. In the beginning, however, a mother needs to be there: she has to be available, attentive, and responsive to her baby. A woman, after all, has to allow herself to become a mother first before she can become a so-called working mother. And becoming a mother takes time. This does not mean that looking after her children is all that she will ever do or be able to do.

I had a wonderful pregnancy with our first child. I was fit and healthy, my skin was pink and glowing, I swam and did pregnancy aerobics several times a week and cycled several miles between home and work every weekday up to and including the day I went into labour. And I liked being on the verge of motherhood, no doubts, no fears plagued me. But for my husband's occasional bouts of morning sickness, I would have happily continued pregnant for years. Then our daughter arrived only two days 'late' after only seven hours of labour, in a birthing pool in a dimly lit room, with the help of my husband and my favourite midwife and some aromatherapy oils, no pain killers, no stitches, no doctors needed. During my labour in the pool, we even had a Japanese tourist drop in to take some photos of me.[16] Obviously, I was made for this. Or not.

As soon as I had delivered the baby, the ambiguity started. I was too exhausted, frankly, to be interested in our baby and was very glad that my husband was there to hold her after the birth. I did not want to hold our baby. I felt disconnected from this little creature who looked at me in such an imperious manner. And then I had to learn everything, everything! That tiny bottom, those many folds, that bizarre excrement, that odd-looking navel, this unfathomable art of latching-on, this insatiable appetite, this distressing cry. It was during our very first night together that I ended up passing our daughter on to the night nurses to get a bit of a break and some sleep.

It has been said that you become a mother only through skin contact with your baby. I think I became a mother thanks to my sense of smell. Each of our babies smelled different and their smells changed over the months but I found each smell absolutely addictive. I wanted to cuddle up to our babies and nuzzle them all the time simply to smell them! (We did not bathe our babies very often, only once or twice a week, which will have helped to keep them deliciously smelly.) It was, therefore, our firstborn's smell which helped to motivate me to stay close to her and as I stayed close to her, I was, of course, there for her and able to get to know her. And as I got to know our daughter, smell and all, I began to find mothering her much easier and therefore was happier being there for her. And so I took my time with mothering – and what a lot of time it took! And eventually I fell in love with our daughter. And that was my lovely loop. My love for our daughter and her little life grew and blossomed together. In the midst of the stresses and strains of young motherhood, I began to feel a deep joy. And it is the joy that has lasted.

II. The transformations wrought by being there in the baby are, to my mind, most wonderful to observe. It is, after all, nothing less than unconditional love which we communicate through being there. By being available, we communicate acceptance. By being attentive, we communicate respect. And by being responsive, we communicate our interest and concern to our baby. As God's "eternal and indestructible love [...] assures the life of each one of us a permanent meaning", so our being there for our child communicates to our child our conviction that "your life is good, even if I don't know your future".[17] And unconditional love is, as we have seen, incredibly powerful: God's love for us makes us lovable. And a mother's love for her baby makes her baby lovable.

I had a terribly keen sense of potential with each of our babies. These skinny and easily outraged little creatures could go either way, I thought; there was no guarantee that they would thrive. I also had a quite overwhelming desire to help our babies to like this world they had been born into, to give them reasons to like it. That then, as I saw it, instinctively, perhaps, was my immediate task: to set our babies on the track to health and happiness. So I concentrated on being there even when, at times, I did not feel like it. It seemed to me a matter of now or never as well as a matter of life and death. I only relented somewhat when, after some weeks, the skinny and easily outraged little creatures had turned into robust and chirpy little characters. And by that time, I was hooked.

There are, first of all, the measurable benefits of being there for your baby. Faster weight gain, greater alertness, and higher levels of activity in babies as well as long-term better general health, increased immunity to illness, and greater intelligence in children have all been linked to the mothers' being there in the beginning. Touch, for example, directly affects the rate at which premature babies gain weight; babies who are stroked regularly gain weight more quickly. Frequently talking to a baby increases the baby's intelligence. And sharing books with babies gives them a head start with reading as well as other school subjects later on. It is not merely the activities of touching, talking, or reading to a baby that matter, however, it is also how these activities are performed that matters. If the activities are performed with understanding of the particular baby and love for the baby, the positive effect is greatest. Which is why there is no real substitute for the mother's being there. Health and intelligence, moreover, are in this context necessarily relative to your child's given potential. One of the healthiest and most intelligent children I know, for instance, is a little boy in the neighbourhood who has Downs' Syndrome. He has made fantastic strides since birth, overcoming obstacles with alacrity. And what he may lack in health and intelligence in absolute terms, he more than makes up for with well above average happiness! It cheers me up simply to look at him.

And then there are the immeasurable benefits of being there for your baby, and these benefits are immeasurable indeed! Through being there for her baby, a mother learns with time to read her baby's verbal and non-verbal signals. This enables a mother – unlike, for example, a nursery nurse at a crèche who has to look after several babies whom she has, moreover, not known from birth – to provide a customised response to her baby's needs and personality. It is as a result of this harmonised interaction, and as a result of the love and understanding expressed through it, that your baby learns that this is a world in which her needs are met and her personality is recognised and accepted. And this experience, in turn, prompts your baby to develop trust in the world around as well as self-confidence. Trust in the world and self-confidence make for a secure baby. And a secure baby is ready to learn, ready to explore, ready to make friends, ready to delight in her own achievements, and ready to delight in what she encounters. A secure baby is ready to take on the world, and that is just as well, for the world is waiting.

Think, if you like, of your being there in the beginning as an investment in your child's and your own future. If you give and take the time now, when your child is a baby, you can get away with giving a lot less later; a good start is half the race. By focusing your effort on your child's health and happiness at the beginning you incidentally work towards your own long-term convenience. Focusing on your own convenience at the beginning, however, puts at risk your child's health and happiness and, therefore, your own long-term convenience. An unwell or unhappy child is, simply put, a lot more work. There seems to be a curious notion out there that mothering involves continuous 100 per cent concentration on your children and is therefore too dull a job for anybody who appreciates mental stimulation. What nonsense! First of all, dullness is a fault rarely encountered in children. Secondly, given their incredible exhaustion and the need to cope with culture shock, mothers of young babies can generally manage quite well without much additional mental stimulation. Thirdly, mothering after the throes of early babyhood is a lot less concentrated affair. Mothers who have been there – who have been, that is, available and attentive and responsive to their babies – can and do engage in all sorts of activities as they mother, only some of which have to do with their children, because their children no longer require their constant attention. Being there in the beginning means you can be somewhere else some of the time later on *without needing to worry.* This is the paradox at the heart of the lovely loop: by being there for your child, you render your child capable of being without you. And enabling your child to be without you is, after all, what your job as a mother is ultimately about.

Staying there

Despite the paradox at its heart, it is wise never to let go entirely of the lovely loop. Being there with your baby provides a sound foundation for your identity as a mother, for your relationship with your child, and for your child's life. As your child grows up, it is helpful to continue to build on that foundation, to touch base, as it were. For one thing, parents need to get to know their children almost continuously as children can change rapidly and as their experiences can differ radically from one day to the next. If you loved your beautiful, burbling baby, chances are you will love the spotty, stroppy teenager your baby has become, but it may take additional effort. Crises, in particular, are times when you need to be there for your child. Caress, for instance, helps to relieve stress. Any illness or distress in any of our children invariably recalls me to the job of being there. My first impulse, in fact, is to sit the child in question on my knee and hum a soothing melody. Regular and age-appropriate being there, however, carries the greatest benefits for your child and your relationship.

Being there for children often is a matter of being in the background. You, alone among childcare providers, do not have to tick boxes concerning your child's development; you do not have to ensure that your four-year-old covers all areas of learning in a given period and produces presentable products to take home as proof. As a mother you can therefore give your four-year-old the time and the space to let his imagination take him wherever he will. And children need that time and space. Children need the freedom to learn to occupy themselves without adult input, and they need the freedom to develop their own imagination. Children need the freedom to create their own worlds before they are absorbed by ours; they need to fight with dragons and dance with fairies before they are taken up by a near seamless round of school lessons and afternoon activities. Through their imaginative play, young children interact with reality on their own terms and try out different identities and possibilities. In the process, they develop their personalities and have great fun. Stand back, watch, or join in – and be fascinated. Children's worlds are incredibly rich worlds, and our world is enriched if we allow children the freedom to develop theirs'.[18]

Being there for your child at any age also means listening, which is a skill all its own. Active listening involves maintaining eye contact at the same level and occasionally acknowledging briefly what you have heard as well as reflecting your child's feelings back to her to make sure you understood correctly.[19] Active listening is always appropriate but particularly so when your child is upset. Active listening shows your child that you accept her and her feelings. This helps your child to express her feelings as well as, eventually and, if necessary, with help from you, to think constructively about the situation upsetting her. Because of the vital importance of communication between you and your child, anger should never be allowed to interfere with it for any length of time. It is therefore important to isolate anger, that is, to recognise that you or your child are angry about a particular incident or behaviour rather than angry about each other as people. And it is similarly important to clear the air before bedtime; anger tended keeps a relationship from being mended. I have found that praying together with our children in the evenings gives us all the chance to let the day pass review – to express gratitude for what we enjoyed, as well as sorrow for the mistakes we made, and our hopes for the next day – and so helps us to continue to listen to each other and be there for each other.

Being there for your children, being available, attentive, and responsive, presents new challenges as they get older. Your fourteen-year-old may not be inclined to gaze at you in rapture nor will he accept cuddles without embarrassment, both of you, moreover, may well be too busy to find much time for each other, but there are still lots of ways of being there for him. I have found that walking rather than driving to and from places gives me precious time with my children. Working together in the kitchen also gives me the chance to spend time with an older child on their own, without the siblings about, which is important. In addition, I usually cut up and distribute pieces of fruit at some point in the afternoon which is equally popular with the big children and the little ones and gives us all the opportunity for a chat. Preparing food for your children and sharing it with them generally is a good way of expressing your love for your children and creating intimacy. And reading a book aloud at bedtime to an older child (I read to our ten-year-old) ensures the two of you have regular time together as well as a shared interest. The casual nature of these encounters and the shared focus on a task, food, or a book help older children to open up. As before, you need to listen closely and respond sensitively by reflecting your children's feelings rather than storming in with your solutions (difficult if, like me, you always know best). The most important thing here is not to solve your children's problems but to communicate your love, to show your children that you care for them, are interested in them, and enjoy spending time with them. Children who feel loved, cared for, and appreciated have the confidence to acquire new skills and engage with others and are, therefore, generally equipped to solve their own problems. You give your children roots and, in time, they grow their wings themselves.

My mother died three weeks after I had signed the contract to write this book. I lost the body that bore and nourished me, my forever reference point, my backbone. The death of a mother, even when you are, as I was, forty years old, is a wrench from security, another birth. The one person who would, I knew, go out of her way for me, who would die for me, had died. There is a sense of fantastic loneliness in that realisation.

Our relationship had not been easy. But approaching death chased away our issues and our wariness and allowed me to see the soul that He had made. I saw my mother's beauty and her courage. I saw her kindness and her infinite generosity. I saw her undying sense of humour. And I saw my mother's sorrow and her need. This was a blessing of the final days.

Approaching death also slowed my mother down. Since my parents' marriage break-up when I was quite small, my mother had resumed her university studies and worked as a secondary school teacher and run a large household and kept open-house for everybody and anybody and looked after my siblings and me and a series of dogs and cats. She also had, or so it had seemed to me, busied herself with busyness: she was forever rushing off to destinations and jumping to conclusions. But at the end, her terrible cancer wore her out and she finally sat still. Just as her time was running out, my mother once again took time and gave time: she was available and attentive and responsive. And I loved it.

NOTES

1 This is *not* a recommendation! Besides, it didn't work.
2 Daniel N. Stern, *The Birth of a Mother* (London: Bloomsbury, 1998) p. 52.
3 Second Vatican Council, *Gaudium et spes*, p. 24.
4 Pope Benedict XVI, *Deus Est Caritas*, p. 18.
5 Pope Benedict XVI, *The Anthropological Foundation of the Family (Part 1)*, Address to the Congress of the Diocese of Rome, June 9, 2005.
6 B. Garrigou-Lagrange, O.P., *The Three Ways of the Interior Life* (Rockford, Illinois: Tan Books, 1977) p. 9.
7 *You saw how the Lord carried you as if you were a child.* Moses, Deuteronomy.
8 Pope Benedict XVI, *Deus Caritas Est*, p. 7.
9 For further information on as well as help with breastfeeding see www.laleche.org.uk
10 A little known fact is that the concentration of lysozyme, an important component of breastmilk which boosts the immune system, actually increases over the first 24 (!) months of breastfeeding,

reaching concentrations in breastmilk as high as those found in colustrum, the thick, yellowish liquid secreted immediately after delivery, *Kidsgo!* (Hamburg, Germany), March 2005.

11 The *Wilkinet Baby Carrier.*

12 What am I doing while writing this? Breastfeeding, of course!

13 Bouncy chairs or seats of any description confine your baby's movements too much. A sling does so as well, of course, but makes up for it with other advantages.

14 And leave them to it! Don't interfere unless absolutely necessary. They, like you, can only get to know your baby and learn how to be with him by being there for him. (I became so convinced of this that, by the time our fourth child was born, I would automatically *leave the room* as soon as the baby was happily settled in somebody else's arms.... "Come back here, Mum!")

15 I wonder whether post-natal depression may, in part, constitute an attempt at such a retreat. Depression is certainly common among people suffering from culture shock.

16 Actually, a Japanese midwifery student taking – modest – photos for a Japanese midwifery magazine.

17 Pope Benedict XVI, address from a ship on the Rhine River to young people gathered in Cologne for World Youth Day, 18 August 2005.

18 You will have surmised that I consider sending four-year-olds to full-time school a bad idea.

19 The course book *From Pram to Primary School* (Family Caring Trust, 1995) by Michael and Terri Quinn provides excellent advice on communicating with children.

4

forgiving

Forgiving is the social aspect of mothering. It is represented by the third circle of the model of mothering. Our ability as mothers to forgive our children flows from our ability as mothers to love our children, and it communicates that love.

Early one morning, Jesus went to the temple and sat down and taught the people who had come to him. The scribes and the Pharisees brought a woman who had been caught in adultery, and placing her in the midst they said to him, "Teacher, this woman has been caught in the act of adultery. Now, in the law Moses commanded us to stone such. What do you say about her?" This they said to test him, that they might have some charge to bring against him. Jesus bent down and wrote with his finger on the ground. And as they continued to ask him, he stood up and said to them, "Let him who is without sin among you be the first to throw a stone at her." And once more he bent down and wrote with his finger on the ground. But when they heard it, they went away, one by one, beginning with the eldest, and Jesus was left alone with the woman standing before him. Jesus looked up and said to her, "Woman, where are they? Has no one condemned you?" She said, "No one, Lord." And Jesus said, "Neither do I condemn you; go, and do not sin again."[1]

As I sit here at my desk, William Blake's depiction of the scene described above looks down on me. Jesus is drawing in the sand.[2] We only see the backs of the men in the crowd; they are already leaving. Jesus' few words clearly have brought about a significant change in them. Only a few moments ago they were raring to trip up Jesus and stone the woman. Now they are walking away from their intended victims. Jesus' words have prompted them to look inward and face a fundamental fact about themselves: we are sinners, each and every one of us. Temporarily, and in the face of others' grave sins, we may, on occasion, appear just and good to ourselves. But when we encounter God, He leads us to see ourselves as we truly are: constitutionally inclined to fall radically short of God's plan for us.[3] And when we know ourselves to be sinners, we know that we are not fit to condemn others.

Jesus does not spell out this progression of realisations to the crowd. Like a wise mother who is keen to teach her children not only to behave but also to think, Jesus merely sets his listeners on the right path and relies on their intelligence to guide them to the necessary conclusion. The men in the crowd were self-righteous and disposed to vengeful violence until Jesus spoke. His words rendered them first thoughtful, and then insightful. When the men in the crowd accepted Jesus' authority, based, as it is, on his superior understanding of human nature, they realised their own sinfulness. They got off their high horses and walked away, implicitly forgiving the woman her offence. Humility before God is always enabling. Here, it enabled the men to understand themselves better, and it enabled them to forgive. They are on their way to becoming better men for their greater understanding of themselves as well as their new-found capacity to forgive and offer others that second chance they themselves, like us, demand daily from God.

The woman in the picture is looking at Jesus as he is drawing in the sand. Perhaps she is wondering whether he

– being, as he is, without sin – will pick up a stone. But we know what happens next. Jesus says to the woman, "Woman, where are they? Has no one condemned you?" She replies, "No one, Lord." And Jesus says, "Neither do I condemn you; go, and do not sin again." Jesus does not throw stones. He does not even condemn the woman. But he does not simply dismiss her, either. He says, "Go, and do not sin again." The woman is free to go, but not free to continue to sin. And there we have the crucial distinction which is central to Christian morality: the distinction between the sin and the sinner. God abhors sin; God loves the sinner. God rejects sin, but embraces the sinner. In Blake's picture, both Jesus and the woman wear white robes and their hair colour and face shapes resemble each other's; they look like brother and sister. God is that close to sinners.

Jesus' words to the woman, like his words to the crowd of men, are stunning in their profound and life-changing simplicity. His words to the woman are full of hope for her. He is telling the woman that she can go *and let go* of her sinful past, that she can start afresh. He sets her free, literally and metaphorically. Simply by commanding her not to sin again, Jesus at once gives the woman's life a new and better orientation and expresses his confidence in her ability to change and live up to that new and better orientation. By distinguishing the sin from the sinner, the act of adultery from the woman, Jesus helps the woman to dissociate herself from her past behaviour. He does not, by accusing or judging her, put the woman into a position in which she feels called upon to explain or defend herself and thus necessarily comes to identify herself more closely with her sin. Instead, Jesus helps the woman to recognise her sinful behaviour for what it is, leave it behind, and move on to a new and better life. Her encounter with Jesus not only saved the woman from stoning, it also saved her years of psychotherapy.

The crowd's forgiveness of the woman depended on

95

their new-found humility and self-awareness. Jesus' for-giveness of the woman goes a step further than theirs: it is an expression of love. In forgiving the woman, Jesus shows her not only that he will not judge her but also that he wants her to live, and to live well. The great and awful truth is that God loves the sinner – that God loves us – and love cannot bear to see the beloved marred or injured. Love necessarily "demands the perfecting of the beloved"; while it "may forgive all infirmities and love still in spite of them […] Love cannot cease to will their removal."[4] God wants us to live, and to live well. And it is God's forgiving love, His loving forgiveness, which together with His law or moral framework enables us to live, and to live well.

I am inclined simply to repeat the passage from St John's Gospel cited above again and again in this chapter, like a mantra. The truth and beauty and wisdom contained in it would thereby, I expect, penetrate the most recalcitrant recesses of our minds and hearts – and then we would know all there is to know about forgiving. As I am unlikely, however, to earn either praise or money for the effort, I have decided to take a different approach to the topic of this chapter: I shall tease apart some of the significance of forgiving and look at that significance specifically as it relates to mothering. In this endeavour, the passage cited above will be my light and inspiration, and I do highly recommend it for meditation.

God and mothers

The Church does its best to communicate the truth, beauty, and wisdom of God's loving forgiveness to us and encourages both the seeking and the granting of forgiveness at every opportunity. At the beginning of Mass, for example, the members of the congregation collectively acknowledge that they have sinned and ask for each other's prayers. In addition, the prayer that Jesus taught his disciples, The

Lord's Prayer, is prayed at every Mass. It contains the pivotal line "forgive us our trespasses as we forgive those who trespass against us".[5] "Whoa!", I think to myself, "am I the measure of God here? Is He to forgive me as I forgive others? Well, I had better get forgiving, then!" And the focal point of Mass is, of course, Jesus' death on the cross where he died *so that our sins may be forgiven.* My petty self-justifications regularly[6] dissolve in the face of such a gift of self, given out of love and for forgiveness.

The Church also encourages the daily examination of conscience. Even a brief examination of conscience can cover all manner of sins of thought, word, deed, or omission, including pride, rudeness, rash judgment, self-pity, greed, and carelessness. An examination of conscience confronts us with ourselves, with only God as witness. There is no need for excuses in this context, only honesty is required. A good examination of conscience inspires sorrow in us for the sins we have committed and leaves us determined, with God's help, to avoid sin in the future. Frequent examination of conscience helps us to keep the divine light switched on, as it were, as we steer our way through muddy waters. By frequently recalling our need for forgiveness for specific sins, we keep in mind our God-given agenda and refuse to allow the agendas of the moment – this whim, that desire, these strains, those stresses – to determine who we are. An unrepented sin, on the other hand, makes us more likely to sin again. Aristotle taught that "the good act perfects the person who does it and the bad act makes the person who does it more imperfect". With practice, the daily examination of conscience enables us to do better and to become better; it enables us to keep a constant eye on the perfect light, and to follow it. For forty days each year during Lent, moreover, the Church sponsors a major retuning effort, as it were, and encourages all Christians to focus on repenting their sins, growing closer to God, and atoning for the evil and misfortune in the world by giving to those in need.

And then there is the Sacrament of Confession or Reconciliation. Yes, this business of forgiving is important enough to warrant its own sacrament. The Sacrament of Confession brings us face to face with our sins and helps to release us from them. In preparing for confession, we examine our thoughts, words, and deeds, and consider how we have sinned. In confession itself, we state clearly and simply what our sins have been. The priest suggests ways to improve and a penance. We then promise to try, with God's grace, not to sin again. Finally, God absolves us of our sins. As we leave the confessional, we leave behind the need to justify our sins as well as the need to repeat them in an attempt to assert ourselves.

> Every contrite confession is a drawing near to the holiness of God, a rediscovery of one's true identity, which has been upset and disturbed by sin, a liberation in the very depth of one's self and thus a regaining of lost joy, the joy of being saved.[7]

God's forgiveness helps us to look on our sins as what they are, without the blinkers of ego-investment. Our experience of God's forgiveness enables us critically to examine our attitudes and actions, acknowledge our mistakes, and to recognise the damage our sins do to our relationship with God, to others, and to ourselves. Our experience of God's forgiveness enables us to distance ourselves from our sins because we know that – with God's help – we can leave wrong ways behind and are free to change for the better. That change requires our own effort as well as, ideally, the assistance of a spiritual advisor, but we, not unlike the alcoholic who finally admits that he has a problem, have taken the crucial first step in the right direction.

The practice of confession reminds us that we are in constant need of forgiveness. Our recognition of our own sinfulness and our experience of God's abiding love for us, in turn, help us to forgive others. God's love is "love which forgives".[8] God loves us despite our sins; God is forever ready to forgive us and help us to overcome our failings. And we are asked to love and forgive others as God loves and forgives us. We, too, must distinguish between the sin and the sinner and keep our love and hope for the sinner intact even as we suffer under the sin committed. We must offer advice and assistance to the sinner, when appropriate, or else wait in prayer and patience for his conversion. We cannot allow our pain or pride to come between us and the sinner, because the sinner, more than anyone, needs our love. Like the father in the parable of the Prodigal Son, we must welcome the sinner with open arms and thereby help to restore him to his real self which is, after all, made in the image of God.

Interestingly, forgiveness frees not only the sinner to change for the better, it also frees the offended party from the destructive force of sin. Focusing on our hurt, cultivating anger, or harbouring resentment damages the self as well as relationships. Unfortunately, I rather like harbouring resentment. Resentment is, after all, such a convenient excuse for failing to put more effort into a relationship. By concentrating on the faults of others, moreover, I can avoid confronting my own shortcomings and my need to ask others for forgiveness. But letting go of resentment and forgiving others is a significant and necessary step towards freedom. As long as I cannot forgive, I am stuck in the past and define myself vis-à-vis others and their actions. When I forgive, however, I free myself from a worrisome past, can begin to concentrate on changing my own behaviour, and open the door to reconciliation. Forgiving heals the self and relationships.

> We imitate God, we live by God, like God, by entering into Christ's manner of life. [...] Paul lists the ways in which we live as God does: "Let all bitterness and wrath and anger and clamour and slander be put away from you, with all malice, and

be kind to one another, tender-hearted, forgiving one another, as God in Christ forgave you." It is by these little daily virtues, again and again, that we step out of our bitterness, our anger towards others, our refusal to accept the other's otherness; by them, again and again, we open up to each other in forgiveness.[9]

Forgiving, like asking for forgiveness, allows us to let go of sin and of our reactions to sin. But forgiving is not instantaneous; it is necessarily a process. Whether we feel resentment, pain, anger, or confusion as the result of another's actions, we are unlikely to be able to overcome these feelings quickly or easily. It is useful, however, to have this goal ahead of us as we are experiencing strong negative emotions. Forgiving is the light at the end of the tunnel; the light towards which we are striving despite the darkness surrounding us. And as we struggle to make progress, it is helpful to keep in mind what forgiving can accomplish, in us and in the other, and in our relationship. Forgiving makes new beginnings possible; forgiving helps us to initiate a better future.

Mothers, above all, are called upon to emulate God's loving forgiveness. Our children need to know that we can draw a distinction between them and their actions, that we will never judge them although we will often have to judge their actions. Our children need to know that they can make mistakes and still return to our embrace; that they can learn from experience and then take that experience to us for our feedback. Our children need to know, moreover, that we have high expectations of them and their behaviour, that we will not settle for easy compromise; and they need to know that we will love them as they try and fail and try again to meet those expectations. And our children need to know that our expectations of them derive from our love for them.

For a time our eldest son considered correction offensive. Whenever I corrected him, he would shut down all receptors or else respond with bathos – "all right, then, if I have to be quiet now, I'll never speak another word in my life!" As a result, I caught myself judging him to be incorrigible, a judgment which I inadvertently expressed through a tense manner towards him. Our son, of course, picked up on my negative attitude and reacted with even greater obstinacy. And so our relationship became increasingly fraught and I felt at a loss as to how to break the vicious circle in which our two personalities were engaged. Then I remembered to pray. I prayed specifically for our eldest son. As I entrusted him to God's care, I managed to let go of my negative judgment of him and to focus instead on my love for him. My approach towards him relaxed, and my hope for him and for our relationship increased. And our son responded to that hope with renewed goodwill.

"We will become what we think we are."[10] And what we mothers say about our children and how we interact with our children are our children's main source of data as to who they are. As long as I communicated to our son my negative expectations, therefore, he did not stand much of a chance of improving his behaviour. My main failure was to equate our son with his behaviour. Because I found his behaviour difficult, I judged our son to be difficult. Only when I realised through prayer that it was not my job to judge our son but to love him, was I able to guide our son by spending time with him and by praising him whenever he behaved considerately. "It is easier to encourage a strong point than to correct a fault!"[11] Children respond to our good opinion of them. It is therefore very much worth our while to let our children know our good opinion of them! And to keep our good opinion of our children intact, we at times need to be able to forgive readily.

Mothers are also called upon to seek the forgiveness of their children. Both, the giving and the asking for forgiveness are essential to mothering. Our children need to know that we are not perfect and they need to know that we know that we are not perfect. Our children need to witness us facing up to our faults. They need to understand that the struggle with sin is just that, a struggle, and a struggle, moreover, which we do not outgrow. Our children need to realise that we are not willing to settle either on the sofa of self-satisfaction or in the ditch of despair but that we keep both the struggle and the hope alive that we can be who we should be. And our children need to understand that we believe that God knows who we should be. Our children, moreover, need to learn to forgive others, and what better way to learn to forgive others than to practise with their mothers!

I often ask our children for forgiveness. I doubt that any of them are impressed by my efforts to improve but at least they know that I am aware of my faults and that I am trying to avoid them and make amends for them. Because I apologise and ask for their forgiveness when I have lost my temper, for example, our children learn that shouting is not a good way to deal with provocation.[12] I, in turn, do not find myself justifying behaviour which I know to be unjustifiable for the sake of appearing authoritative. Rather than engaging in a show of power over our children by assuming an attitude of self-righteousness, I acknowledge that I wronged them. And our older children, God bless them for it, turn into spiritual advisors and suggest that, next time, I count till ten or leave the room for a while before reacting to a perceived impertinence. (I, of course, suggest that they help me to avoid the near occasion of sin by behaving respectfully at all times.) Our children will be much better adults than me, I am sure, not least because my mistakes, those which mothering has helped me to become aware of, at any rate, are on the table, uncovered, to be weighed and analysed, and avoided.

When I rearranged our twelve-year-old daughter's violin lesson with her teacher one morning for that afternoon, our daughter was very annoyed with me as she had made other plans. It took me a while to realise that I had been wrong in failing to consult her. By the time our daughter came down to the kitchen to give me a forgiving hug, however, I was ready to apologise. I had assumed that she would not have had any other plans and the incident helped me to realise that she had grown more independent. Without our daughter's loving gesture of forgiveness, or the prospect of it, the chances are that I may have hardened rather than softened my position which would have created distance in our relationship – and left me with a flat learning curve.

As mothers, then, we need to be able to forgive as well as to ask for forgiveness. If we remain close to God's love and follow His forgiving example, we can learn to do both. The practice of forgiving and asking for forgiveness helps to increase our understanding of ourselves and of our children and helps us and our children to change for the better. The practice of forgiving and asking for forgiveness also teaches us and our children that relationships continue, that relationships can, in fact, get better, after conflict, after error and hurt. The practice of forgiving and asking for forgiveness, moreover, gives us peace – peace with God, peace with the past, peace with ourselves, and peace with our children. The mother-child relationship thrives on mutual forgiving.

Mothers and morals

Forgiving communicates redeeming love. Forgiving allows us and others to grow in understanding and holiness. And forgiving helps us to develop loving, lasting relationships. It is an immense pity, therefore, that forgiving is well on the way to becoming a lost art. This is not the case because we find it increasingly difficult to tolerate sin, be it that of others or our own. On the contrary, we are now living in a thoroughly tolerant society. In fact, we have become so tolerant that we hardly sin any more. No, forgiving is not becoming a lost art because we cannot tolerate sin any longer. It is becoming a lost art because we increasingly lack anything to forgive. To forgive others and to seek forgiveness we need something to forgive, and to have something to forgive we need to hold on to the concept of sin as well as, and here is the real stumbling block, to values besides the values of tolerance, choice, and self-interest.

Tolerance, a noble ideal, has been abused to make a mockery of itself; it has bitten itself in the tail and is about to devour the rest. We are so incredibly tolerant now that there is little to tolerate as we are under pressure only to pass on watered-down, lowest-common-denominator, one-size-fits-all values that leave all options open. As a result, an apparently tolerant attitude these days is more likely to be due to indifference than to conscientious wrestling with difference. In fact, the moral maxims of the day may be summed up in the axiom *you can do what you like as long as you let me do what I like* – choice and self-interest. And that is not good enough. Such a limited value system may be adequate for some purposes (though I doubt it, as those purposes would ultimately flounder for lack of purpose). It is, however, not a moral framework or value structure capable of supporting mothers in their mothering.

As mothers we need a comprehensive value structure to pass on to our children. As mothers, after all, we have to point out the limits of the tolerable before we encourage our children to exercise tolerance. We have to educate our children before we allow them to choose. We have to teach our children about their responsibilities before we hand them their rights. We have to make our children aware of the interests of others before we let them pursue their own interests. And we have to explain to our children the value of commitment before we give them their freedom. As mothers, moreover, we need to raise our children with real, lived-in values that call for expression in actual behaviour such as praying, telling the truth, treating others with respect and consideration, helping at home and in the community, giving generously, avoiding waste, asking for forgiveness, and forgiving! Polite nodding in the direction of a vague ideal will not catch the imagination nor inspire the commitment of our children, nor will the values of choice and self-interest – except to engender egotism. The current dominance of so-called youth culture in which everybody from the six-year-old to the sixty-year-old is encouraged to emulate the careless self-centredness of the morally undereducated sixteen-year-old is symptomatic of a historically unique wholesale abnegation of responsibility.

As soon as our children are properly mobile, they require a framework in which to move. Such a framework is mainly communicated by means of rules, and I am referring here not to rules which keep our children from bumping their heads but to rules which help to guide our children's experience in a broad sense. Children need rules which help them: 1. to discover the world, 2. to engage with the world, and 3. to understand the world and their place in it. The values of choice and self-interest cannot provide a framework which does any of this. Christian values, on the other hand, do just the job. Christian values may not seem convenient at all times, but they are inspired by, and expressive of, truth, beauty, and wisdom. And a concern for truth, beauty, and wisdom, rather than a concern with convenience, is what will lead our children to full human maturity.[13] Christian values guide our children so that they can come to trust in the goodness of their own lives and the relationships that constitute them; so that they can trust the validity of their commitment to build with others something in common.[14]

Guided discovery. It tickles me no end when parents lay claim to enlightenment because they do not bring up their children in a faith, purportedly so that their children "can choose for themselves what is right for them". Given the nature of society around us, these children are as likely to become vegetable gardeners or opera buffs as committed believers without the gentle insistence of their parents that they go and discover what is less than immediately obvious or desirable but nonetheless worthwhile, and stick at it. There is a fascinating world out there, a world of many splendours, and if we leave it entirely up to our children where to tread, the chances are they will not discover more than a tiny percentage of it, nor will they discover the rewards of perseverance. It is easier, much easier, of course, to avoid conflict and the risk of rejection and let our children decide for themselves what to eat for dinner, to take one familiar situation. Our children will, however, almost certainly not base their decision on some independent inner light but on the last junk food advertisement they saw. And we know how limiting that will be to their enjoyment of good food and, ultimately, to their enjoyment of good health. No, children need years and years of gentle but insistent guided discovery so that, eventually, they are able to make genuine decisions based on a large repertoire of varied, valuable, in-depth experiences.

Guided engagement. Children are not born knowing principles of engagement with others; they need to be taught these. Children, moreover, *want* to be taught how to engage with others. Guiding rules of behaviour, although often a challenge, are also, and just as often, a source of reassurance. Rules of behaviour help children to deal with new or difficult situations. When we teach our children to consider other people's needs, for example, they will eventually learn to look beyond themselves. And that is a good thing in itself as well as a fine way to avoid social awkwardness which more often than not arises from an exaggerated concern with oneself. Rules of behaviour also help children to develop self-control, and a child's self-control benefits the child at least as much as it benefits others. Rules of behaviour, moreover, delimit a child's boundaries. A lack of boundaries places too much responsibility on children and leaves them disoriented and subject to sundry influences. A sense of boundaries drawn by benign and wise authority, on the other hand, gives children security and confidence. Teenagers cannot be expected to make their own decisions about sex, for example, as they lack the necessary understanding. We therefore have to communicate to our older children the relevant values, such as the dignity of the person and the most wonderfully untrivial nature of sex, and discuss with them the behavioural implications of those values. Information alone, e.g., on contraception and the prevention of sexually transmitted infections, is counter-productive as it creates the illusion of understanding in young minds, the illusion of being prepared for something for which no amount of information can be sufficient preparation. Only a moral framework, rules and their reasons, can properly prepare teenagers and guide them in this important area of their lives as in so many others.

Guided understanding. Reason is a useful tool but, on its own, incapable of yielding meaning or morals. Reason is necessarily subservient to a given goal and, as mothers, we have to make sure that our children's reason does not serve unworthy masters. Our children need our help in making sense of the world and their place in it. Our children need approaches, if not answers, to the big questions, for these will come up before we know it. Above all, our children need faith for "faith liberates reason from its blind spots [and helps it] to see its proper object more clearly".[15] Faith in God who loves and guides us is at once an *existential comfort* which liberates our reason from the shackles of fear and an *existential challenge* which prompts our reason to search beyond current intellectual conventions for deeper meanings. And our children need both comfort and challenge.

Guided discovery and guided engagement go a long way towards meeting our children's need for meaning. Our own example, moreover, does much to communicate essential values to our children. The importance we attach to worshipping and thanking God, how we draw on our faith for guidance and sustenance, the love and respect we show towards our spouse and our children as well as others, how we respond to others' needs, the way we deal with setbacks, the joy we take in celebrating the Christian feasts, how we contribute to our parishes and communities, how we treat animals, the care we take with our work, the books we read, the stories we tell, how we spend our money and use our free time, all indirectly help to establish a structure of significances in our little ones' minds as they watch and join in. As our children grow up, we do well also to address the search for significance directly. We should share with our children our love for life and Creation, and our faith in life after death. We should talk with them about the hope that God's love for us gives us, even when particular circumstances look hopeless. We should explain to them that loving, while not always easy, is always worthwhile[16], and that forgiving and seeking forgiveness accomplish more than resentment and revenge. We should let them know that the best way to work for their own good is to work for the good of others, and that truth, beauty, and wisdom are worth every inconvenience. Discussions with our older children about possible careers invariably lead me into musings on the meaning of life. Given the context in which we mothers have to work, it is not easy, I have found, to convince impressionable youngsters that good looks, fame, lots of money, and a villa with an indoor as well as an outdoor swimming pool in Spain are not the aims of our existence.[17] But I keep trying to go against the tide of popular superficialities threatening to swamp our children's susceptibilities.

If we manage to complete, as it were, this task of mothering – the transmission of a value structure to our children – our children will leave home with a rich pool of experience to draw on, a well developed conscience, and a firm foundation of faith that will serve them in whatever life throws at them. And society will be better off for them. And the art of forgiving will not be forgotten.

Moral formation

Forgiving, as we have seen, depends on humility and love as well as a value structure. Transmitting values, in turn, requires humility and love as well as forgiving. If we lack humility and refuse to submit ourselves to the moral framework we aim to transmit to our children, our efforts will have very limited success at best and, at worst, make not only ourselves but the entire moral framework appear ridiculous. And if we lack love, we might as well cease all attempts at moral formation as "the key to education is a torrent of love".[18] Communicating our love for our children to our children prepares the field for the task of leading our children towards holiness. We have to feed, as it were, our children with our time and our concern for them as well as with praise for their efforts and achievements if we want our children to grow in virtue. Only if our children know that we love them, will they be inclined to pay attention to, ponder, and respond positively to our attempts to guide them. "The best way to make children good is to make them happy", Oscar Wilde said, and that is essentially the same point. In addition, and apparently paradoxically, our children need to know that we will forgive them should they fall short. Only if our children know that our love for them is unconditional – forever forgiving, persevering and hopeful – can our efforts bear fruit. Only if our children know that they can return to us if they have failed to meet our expectations, will they continue to try to meet our expectations. Only if our children know that we accept them even when we reject what they have done, can they themselves come to reject their errors – and move on.

Love is not only a prerequisite of moral formation, it is also part and parcel of the very process of transmitting values to our children. The process of transmitting values to our children has to be finely tailored to our children's physical, emotional, mental, and spiritual readiness to try new tasks and learn new lessons. Transmitting values to our children therefore requires spending time with our children, time in which we talk to them and listen to them, pray together, eat together, play games with them, and work side by side with them. Transmitting values to our children requires us to share goals with our children, express our expectations of our children, praise our children for their efforts, give good example, explain our actions, and show our children that we trust them to do what is right. Transmitting values to our children requires us to be available, attentive, and responsive to our children; transmitting values to our children, in other words, requires us to be there. And being there, we know, is not a matter of short bursts of activity-laden so-called quality time now and again. Given the need for an approach marked by love and understanding as well as coherence and continuity, the job of transmitting values to our children cannot be left to strangers.

The moral formation of our children, then, is a labour which requires believing, loving, and forgiving. It is therefore a job for which mothers are eminently well qualified. And thank God for that, because the moral formation of our children is a job that has got to be done and one that has got to be done well. I cannot think of another job anywhere near as important as this particular job. We need mothers to be formative influences for good on their children. We need mothers to embed their children in a value structure that their children can live by and work with. We need mothers to give their children rules and resources. We need mothers. And mothers need all the support they can get. Although mothers can get far with their children by believing, loving, and forgiving, mothers cannot get far enough without the support of others.

Mothers need the support of the government. As it is, the government is helping to separate mothers from their children through pressure, financial and other, on mothers of young children to work outside the home and on fathers as well as mothers to work long hours. The government further works to separate mothers from their children through its appropriation of some of the responsibilities of parents, most notably its ideologically biased sexual health initiatives. Government-sponsored parenting courses are all very well but not a great deal of use when parents have too little time to spend with their children and the school nurse flogs contraceptive advice to twelve-year-olds. The government can choose, however, to offer support, financial and other, to mothers in their mothering and thence in the moral formation of their children. How much easier mothering will be when jobs and taxes allow mothers as well as fathers to spend more time at home![19]

Mothers also need the help of the media. I have a vision of the media selling us truth, beauty, and wisdom, in addition to information, entertainment, and opinion. Specifically, I envision *popular* lives of saints (whoever said that being good was dull has not read any saints' lives), moral self-improvement paperbacks aimed at young people (how about *The Guys' Good Life Guide* and *The Smart Girl's Guide to Being Good*), ethically oriented magazines for young people[20], cool Christian novels for young adults... Any budding C.S. Lewises out there? Get writing! And you media moguls, get publishing and marketing the stuff! I reckon that there is a thirst out there – a gap in the market – amidst the noise and bright lights. Noise and bright lights, and louder noise and brighter lights, can offer only distraction. They are not a substitute for values and beliefs worth living for. I also envision *popular* pop songs with a positive message, celebrity virgins, television sit-coms with believable and inspiring Christian characters in them (and an end to facile, ignorant portrayals of the Catholic Church), and major advertising campaigns promoting ethical shopping habits[21] as well as campaigns promoting spending time with children, our children as well as others', rather than buying things. How would it be if people commonly considered working together with their children in the kitchen or giving a talk at the local school (e.g., 'what my average day as a journalist/MP/mother of five/surgeon/ flight attendant/priest is really like') a greater treat and privilege than owning a home cinema system that matches your own individual interior design specifications?[22] It would be great – for everybody (except home cinema manufacturers). More and more broadly marketed alternatives to lowest-common-denominator values will make the job of mothering, in particular the task of the moral formation of our children, much easier.

Mothers also need the support of playgroups, schools, and youth groups. Given current moral chaos and downright moral dearth, playgroups, schools, and youth groups with an ethical agenda are a godsend. After all, if we mothers are the only people who are educating our children with reference to a moral framework, our children are unlikely to become convinced that that framework is such a good thing. But these playgroups, schools, and youth groups are facing hard times these days, as they face government pressure to water down their values for the sake of that bad joke, that sorry figure, which the value of tolerance has become. I ran a Church of England playgroup for a while, for instance, and recall receiving critical comments from the OFSTED inspector about our practice of singing Grace before snack time.[23] Naughty, naughty us! The government can choose, however, to offer substantial help, financial and other, to playgroups, schools, and youth groups that contribute to the moral formation of our children. When our children encounter in a variety of different settings the same or similar values, rules and reasons, as in the home, it will make our job of mothering and especially the moral formation of our children, a great deal easier.

A brief aside: the biggest challenge to a faith-based moral framework is not a moral framework based on another faith, it is the complete lack of a faith-based moral framework. Committed believers of different faiths all refer to a higher, divine authority which essentially renders their approaches to meaning and morality similar and distinguishes them from those of non-believers. Overt Christian practise in playgroups, schools, or youth groups therefore discriminates less against the beliefs of ethnic minorities than atheistic practice (and I include the popular a-little-bit-of-this-and-a-little-bit-of-that-but-nothing-too-serious approach to religious practice under the heading of atheistic practice). And yet, the government has decided to favour the latter, more discriminatory practice, possibly in the mistaken belief that atheistic practice represents neutral ground.[24] It does not.

Above all, mothers need the support of our immediate and extended families, our friends, and our children's peers. In a sense, every mother in her own way and within her own possibilities has to recreate the village. A village-type community around us is an extremely welcome support in every aspect of mothering but in none more so than in the moral formation of our children. While the nuclear family is the quintessential moral community, the base camp of moral formation, the values of that community need to be reflected in its wider relationships for moral formation to be effective. The family, in other words, needs to reach out to others as well as to be open to the input of others with a similar moral outlook. As mothers, then, we need to gather around us micro-communities in which what other people do and say helps rather than hinders the moral formation of our children. The apparently old-fashioned idea of influencing our children's choice of friends therefore makes good modern sense. It also makes sense to choose our own friends (starting with our husbands!) at least in part on the basis of their values – and then to involve them in our family life! Sharing meals, childcare, pets, projects, celebrations, walks, holidays and more with our extended family and friends creates a community, a community of values, for our children to grow up in and participate in. When our children can experience our moral framework as vibrant, lived-in, and, perhaps most importantly, adaptable to different personalities and circumstances, the moral formation of our children will be much easier.

With a little help from our families and friends, and playgroups and schools and youth groups as well as the media and the government, we can do it. We can raise children who have the capacity to choose good, children who are truly free.[25] What kind of a world do we want? A world which is a home to truth and beauty and wisdom.[26] How do we achieve it? We start with ourselves and what we do, in the family as well as at work, and then teach our children and enrol our communities in the job of teaching our children. And in every instance the best way to begin aiming for what is good is to forgive what isn't.

NOTES

1 John 8:3-11.
2 I enjoy this detail, particularly since becoming a mother: Jesus is taking time to think before he speaks, and giving his listeners time to think after he has spoken. If I could consistently emulate Jesus in this one respect only, much would be gained by my family!
3 That is, subject to original sin.
4 C.S. Lewis, *The Problem of Pain* (London: The Centenary Press, 1945) p. 34.
5 Luke 11:4.
6 My petty self-justifications *regularly* dissolve at Mass because they have a tendency *regularly* to build up again. This is one of several good reasons for frequent Mass attendance.
7 John Paul II, 2/12/84.
8 Pope Benedict XVI, *Deus Caritas Est,* p. 10.
9 Cardinal Joseph Ratzinger, *Many Religions – One Covenant: Israel, the Church and the World*: pp. 84-88.
10 Fernando Corominas, *Bringing up Children Today III* (Madrid: Palabra).
11 Ibid.
12 I am aware that my approach here rather resembles the 'do as I say, not as I do' method of parenting which is rightly out of favour. The difference between my approach and that method, however, is

significant: by admitting my errors and asking for forgiveness I do not place myself above the law but, on the contrary, acknowledge an authority higher than myself to which I, like my children, am subject.

13 For an incredibly insightful book to assist you in leading your children to full human maturity, see David Isaacs, *Character Building* (Blackrock, County Dublin: Four Courts Press, 1993).

14 "Without the light of truth, sooner or later every person is condemned to doubt the goodness of his own life and the relation-ships that constitute it, the validity of his commitment to build with others something in common," Pope Benedict XVI, address delivered from a ship on the Rhine River at the World Youth Day in Cologne, 18 August, 2005.

15 Pope Benedict XVI, *Deus Caritas Est*, p. 28.

16 An inspired book to help you explore this subject with your children is *The Art of Loving Well* (Boston, Mass.: Boston University, 1993).

17 In case you are wondering: the actual aims of our existence are staying a UK Size 12, working through the piles of papers on the floor, mortgage payments which are less than half our monthly income, and a big old house in South Shropshire with land, a stream, and a pond. Only kidding. The aim of our existence is to please God.

18 Fernando Corominas, *Training the Will* (Madrid: Palabra, 1993).

19 And how much likelier parents will be to try to ensure that their children are good company when they start spending significant periods of time with them!

20 There is one, at least: *Tamezin*. For more information contact Tamezin Magazine, 1 Chelsea Embankment, London SW3 4LG, Tel. 020 7352 1545.

21 A recent highlight of my life was when our eldest daughter informed me that 'Fair Trade' was now a fashionable brand. I am not sure the statement makes sense as fair trade is, in part, surely an attempt to get away from the dominance of brands. But it was nice, anyway, to be deemed fashionable rather than peculiar.

22 If you are – but surely you are not – checking this footnote because you are wondering where to get one, I am afraid I have no idea whether such things even exist as I just made it up.

23 Thank you for the world so sweet, thank you for the food we eat, thank you for the birds that sing, thank you, Lord, for everything. Amen.

24 Perhaps, however, the government is motivated rather by a desire to avoid causing offence to the vastly more influential number of atheists. As a result of pressure from atheists, "secularism is no longer that element of neutrality, which opens up space for freedom

for all. It is beginning to change into an ideology which, through politics, is being imposed," Cardinal Ratzinger in an interview with *La Republica*, quoted in *The Catholic Herald*, 22 April 2005.

25 "Freedom is the capacity to choose good," Fernando Corominas, *Bringing up Children Today* (Madrid: Palabra).

26 A somewhat ambitious agenda, I know. I believe in setting our sights high – we might catch a glimpse of God!

5

Persevering

Persevering is the practical aspect of mothering. It is represented by the outermost circle of the model of mothering. Our management of our household and our family builds on and gives expression to our beliefs, our love, and our readiness to forgive.

Here is a television programme waiting to happen. The tasks are many, the time is short. The contestants have to surmount the obstacle course presented by a beckoning household – unpack and put away ten bags of groceries, hang out the washing, answer a phone call from a utility company, repair a torn dress, mop up cat sick, prepare a wholesome meal – to reach a desk where they have to respond to emails and pay bills. Contestants are judged mainly on speed, but also on quality, tidiness, and pleasantness. The winning contestant is crowned home maker of the week and, the following week, has to compete against a new set of contestants completing even more and ever more challenging tasks. The series is open-ended; it continues as long as there are contestants able to compete. Wailing infants, flooding toilets, fighting siblings, implausible homework assignments, cowboy builders and so forth are added to the background arrangements to provide ever-greater levels of difficulty. The series stops when there are no longer any contestants up to the job.

Perhaps this is what it would take. Perhaps television, the great populariser of our time, could achieve what is critically overdue: wide recognition of the skill, knowledge, and, above all, perseverance required to be an effective home maker. Until such a time when we have such a television programme, there is this chapter.

As the largest of the four circles describing mothering, the practical aspect of mothering requires considerable time as well as physical and mental effort. Providing our children with food, clothing, and shelter (pets, transport, piano lessons, holiday activities, birthday parties...) is no mean feat. The practical aspect of mothering is *exhausting*. Since the practical aspect of mothering is the aspect most remote from the centre of mothering, moreover, its significance is often not immediately apparent. When I am cuddling one of our children, I know that I am mothering, when I am dusting radiators, however, I am not so sure. The practical aspect of mothering can seem *trivial*. Thirdly (as though our exhaustion and doubts weren't enough), since the practical aspect of mothering presents the outer edge, as it were, of mothering it exposes mothering to the glare of the world and the shrieks of commerce, "buy me, buy me!" As we stand there – weary, dust rag in hand – we are inundated by a plethora of products and their associated fashions in meal preparation, house cleaning, home decorating, child entertainment, recreation, and what not. The practical aspect of mothering is *under siege*. Help!

To persevere with the practical aspect of mothering – to do the chores, to do them cheerfully, and to keep doing them – we need help indeed. We can, however, help ourselves through what we do and through what we think. There are many techniques and approaches which render this aspect of mothering both less exhausting and more enjoyable. But before we get off the couch and start home managing in earnest, a few general pointers. Broadly speaking, home management consists of two main tasks: managing things and managing people. These two tasks are significantly different and therefore require different strategies. The main difference between the two tasks is that we can control things but cannot, ultimately, control people. Controlling things is essential lest things control us; I imagine you don't want your life to be dominated by concerns about clutter, cleanliness, and the contents of your fridge. The challenge to you, therefore, is to put things in their place, both literally and metaphorically, as well as to consider the wider implications of your actions. Managing people is a different matter. In the household, the people concerned are primarily your children, though your husband and, if applicable, a nanny, an au-pair, a cleaner, as well as workmen will to some extent also come under your direction in your role as home manager. People management requires above all clear expectations and trust. With your children, the believing, loving, and forgiving you have been doing will stand you in very good stead here. The challenge to you is to communicate both your expectations and your trust effectively. Both managing things and managing people have one thing in common, however: they are much easier if you first *think about the principles behind your practice* and then go on to *develop some good working habits*. Once you have done the thinking and developed the habits, you will find that you have plenty of time and energy left to tackle challenges beside and beyond those involved in home management.

What about God? While God is at the centre of our mothering and loves and forgives without bounds and is, as we have seen, our foundation and model for these aspects of mothering, I cannot quite get my head around the image of God as the great home manager in the sky. Perhaps I should. But I expect that heaven pretty much runs itself, which is why it is heaven. God, however, certainly perseveres – boy, does He persevere! At the end of this chapter, therefore, we shall have a look at what it takes to persevere, godlike, with the cleaning, shopping, cooking, washing, organising, insisting etc., etc. We shall also consider the fact that there are times when we cannot manage, and have to surrender.

Managing things

I am not a patient person. In fact, I am probably the least patient person I know: if our two eldest have not done what I want them to do *before* I tell them what it is, I am likely to blow up. Luckily, I am patient with babies and toddlers. Perhaps this is where most of my patience is used up because I have little left for older children, even less for adults (including myself), nearly none for politicians, and none at all for things. The task of managing things therefore presents me with a particular challenge.

I also struggle with the virtue of humility. Paradoxically, humility is one of my favourite virtues; I could hold forth by the hour on the virtue of this virtue. How can we ever learn genuinely new lessons (rather than merely pick up further confirmation of what we think we know) if we lack humility? How can we ever look for and discover the beauty, goodness, and wisdom in others, how can we ever – as the Christian succinctly puts it – see Christ in others without humility? How can we ever discern the will of God if we have no humility? I mention humility not only so that I can indulge in raptures about it but mainly to point out that humility seems a useful virtue to have if you spend much time every day, as I do, in an occupation which is not only unpaid but also considered mindless and monotonous.

Yet, here I am, impatient to an extreme and, alas, more prone to hubris than humility *and* persevering with managing things – and enjoying it. I manage, on the one hand, by making sure that I do as little as possible in the way of managing things while still maintaining fairly high domestic standards. On the other hand, I ensure that what I do in the way of managing things is as interesting and as significant as possible. As it happens, the key elements of this strategy all begin with an 'r' – which is really a great stroke of luck if you are writing a book. They are: *reducing, routine, rethinking, reintegrating, reskilling,* and *resignifying.*

If you adopt them all, I promise you that you, too, will find it a breeze to persevere with managing things.

Reducing. The more you have the more you have to look after. So, get rid of stuff. Here are a few tips to help you on the way. (These tips, incidentally, double as my budgeting advice.) 1. Stop accumulating stuff *now*. Before you go shopping, write a list of items you actually need, then stick to it. The items on the list have to be either useful or beautiful, and ideally both.[1] Be critical in assessing your need as well as the usefulness and beauty of items! Buy only good quality items so as to retrain yourself, if necessary, to appreciate quality rather than quantity. Develop a hobby other than shopping.[2] Nip childhood and adolescent consumer frenzy in the bud by being there for your children; the clutter clearance guru Karen Kingston simply states that "when a child feels loved, secure and happy, they don't have such a reliance on 'things'".[3] 2. To avoid clutter in your fridge as well as waste ensure that all or nearly all the fresh food in your kitchen has been consumed before you buy any more. Shop and cook accordingly. 3. Remove from your home whatever is not useful or beautiful[4] and give these things to friends who do not share your view of them or else to charity[5]. Keep things of sentimental value, by all means, but try not to attach sentimental value to useless or ugly things.[6] 4. Always have a 'charity bag' on the go in which you put anything you notice which seems to have outlived its usefulness in your home. When the bag is full, briefly re-examine its contents, discuss the fate of items with interested parties (I would refrain, however, from consulting very small children as they tend to want what they see), then carry the bag to the nearest charity shop. Your home's supply of toys, in particular, requires regular reviews. If you are unsure about a toy, put it away for a while: if it has not been missed after several weeks, it can go. 5. Circulate children's toys, clothes, and equipment among your circle of friends if you have several children:

pass on what no longer suits your eldest child, noting that you would like it back, if possible, when your second child has reached the appropriate age, etc. 6. Rotate toys within your own home: hide about one third of the toys you still have left after having done all of the above in a cupboard for, say, a couple of months, then get them out and put away the next third, etc. Your children will be delighted by their 'new' toys and there will be less to tidy up. 7. When travelling, pack the minimum. It is good to remind ourselves from time to time how little we need.

Having passed on at least half of your family's possessions you may well think you are done with reducing but there is more, so much more, reducing you can do. Now is the time to reduce the number of chores you do. Consider what matters most to you and your family and what you like doing best, then decide what your priorities are: creating meals, restoring order, or busting grime. All three types of work are necessary to make and maintain a home but you do not have to invest equal amounts of effort in all three. Your energy, like your money, is a limited resource and therefore best spent with deliberation. I myself, for example, consider cooking far more important than tidying, and tidying more important than cleaning[7]. And just as I am happy to spend more money than we can afford on organic food each week but rarely spend any money on clothes or cosmetics, I am happy to spend an hour a day cooking but could not countenance spending that amount of time working to achieve squeaky clean, empty surfaces. There is no single way to go about home making as no two mothers and no two families are alike. Cut corners where you like, therefore, but make sure you all can, in fact, live with the consequences of your decisions.

Routine. When the broad brushstrokes of the when, the how, the where, and the what have become routine, you don't spend your day preoccupied with dull decisions, wasted effort, or tension headaches. A good working routine therefore frees you to do much more than what is prescribed by the routine – and that is the point of a routine. To devise a routine for yourself and your family, you need to consider the timing of actions, the actions themselves, the space in which you do them, and any knowledge relevant to the routine. By another stroke of luck, the first letters of these aspects of your routine spell T-A-S-K. If you take the time to figure out what works best for you and your family, they will also spell E-F-F-I-C-I-E-N-C-Y.

T. Establish a rhythm which corresponds to your requirements and fits in with other activities. I find grotty bathrooms depressing, for example, so I have to make sure that I get to them before they get to me. I clean our bathrooms every Friday which helps to put me in a good mood for the weekend. There is nothing mandatory about a seven-day rhythm, however, though it does make it easier to remember chores if you always do them on the same weekday. Decide whether you prefer clustering or spreading chores. I prefer clustering cleaning jobs, which I dislike, but you may well prefer to do a little and often to stay on top of things. Other jobs, such as changing the bedding, are best spread over several days or weeks as they become unwieldy when clustered; if I change only one or two beds per week rather than the whole lot, the washing machine and I can cope. Tasks like washing up or doing the laundry are best done as soon as – but not before – you have enough dirty dishes to fill a drying rack or enough dirty clothes to fill a washing machine as piles of dirty dishes and overflowing laundry baskets limit space. You also need more dishes and more clothes if you keep many of them dirty and therefore out of use at any one time and, as we have seen, you want less, not more, stuff. Make a list of extraordinary or irregular jobs that need doing, such as ringing the electrician or cleaning the oven, and keep the list where you see it. Begin with the most urgent or, if nothing is particularly urgent, with your least favourite job and cross jobs off the list as you do them. Then start a new list. Also, set aside a time slot for housework and fit the chores you have decided to do into that slot. What does not get done in the allotted time does not get done, tough. (I expect, however, that you will find that you do all the chores, only more quickly.) Housework can, as we all know, expand indefinitely. Don't let it.

A. Develop efficient ways of doing regular chores, such as preparing favourite meals, then stick to them; they'll become second nature and you'll be able to do them with your brain somewhere else in minimum time, which can be useful. Don't answer the phone unless you actually can and want to talk on the phone at that moment. Don't do anything twice if once will do (opening the fridge, walking up or down the stairs, running the washing machine, going shopping…). Leave things you need to remember where you can see them. Double up tasks when you can: put away (air-dried) dishes whenever you wait for the kettle to boil, cooking and washing up can also combine well. Now, I am dying to share with you the most efficient method of washing up, ever, introduced to me by an Austrian friend. Here it is: you put the glasses on their sides into the washing-up bowl as it half fills with water and add some washing-up liquid, you turn off the water. You wash the glasses and put them on a plastic tray next to your washing up bowl. Now you put in the cutlery and plates (which you have already rinsed briefly) into the washing-up bowl. You let these soak as you rinse all the glasses in one go under a running tap and put them on the drying rack. You turn off the water and wash the plates and cutlery and put these on the tray. Now you put the saucepans into the washing up bowl and let them soak as you rinse the plates and cutlery, again all in one go. Then you wash and rinse the saucepans. In this way, you work your way from the cleanest to the dirtiest items to be washed, and should therefore not have to change the washing-up water unless there is an inordinate amount to wash up. You also avoid the waste of time and water involved in turning the tap on and off as you rinse a single item before washing up the next. You allow everything to soak a bit before you tackle it, moreover, which makes it easier to clean. Thank you for paying attention.

S. If you have 'a place for everything and – if you are really lucky – everything in its place', you don't have to think twice about where to find things and where to put things, and that makes home making a lot easier, and a lot quicker. Keys, shoes, lunch boxes, scissors etc. all need their assigned place. Another point about space is that the right space can greatly facilitate a task. If you keep your ironing board, for example, in a room in which you have elbow room to iron as well as space to hang up freshly ironed clothes and in which you keep a radio, as well, (a TV would increase your ironing time) it will make ironing easier to set up and more pleasant to do. Organise your home so as to help you get tasks done efficiently. If you have a choice, ensure that the fridge, the sink, a work surface, and the cooker are proximate to each other as walking across the kitchen or around a table with your arms full of vegetables, the colander, the chopping board, the saucepan can be cumbersome. Find a space for your children to do their homework or practise their instruments in or near the kitchen so that you can supervise their efforts while you are cooking dinner or washing up. Keep a piece of paper and a pen in the same place in the kitchen at all times to note down anything you need to buy *as it occurs to you*. Note items down, moreover, in an order which *corresponds to the lay-out of the shop*, that is, in the order in which you will find them as you pass through the shop. Keep several lists if you do your grocery shopping in several shops.

K. A routine that is set in stone is worse than no routine at all. A routine needs daily tweaking to adjust to changing moods, energy levels, needs, and circumstances and, once in a while, it requires a considered overhaul, a thorough revision, in the light of more dramatic changes, such as a house move, different work or school hours, the introduction of a new gadget (a dishwasher??), and, most dramatically, the arrival of a baby. Consider in advance which aspects of your routine can give so you need not abandon your entire routine when you are under particular strain. I am a cloth nappy[8] devotee, for example, but at times of greater stress I resort to environmentally friendly disposables[9] without guilt-tripping myself. Remain alert to changes that demand a major change in routine. We recently shifted much of our furniture around the house, for instance, to accommodate the changing requirements of our growing children. Life is change. And the point of knowledge is to enable us to adjust.

Rethinking. Effective and enjoyable home making calls for acuteness of observation, lateral thinking, and innovative approaches. Here is food for thought: in China, toddlers wear trousers with slits in the seat, and no nappies. I leave the rest to your imagination. Don't take anything for granted. Does the first floor of your home need vacuum cleaning as frequently as the ground floor? How many items in your family's wardrobe really require ironing? Is the largest bedroom best used by the parents who rarely enter it during the day or might it be better used as a children's bedroom as children need floor space to play with their toys? Do you either have to do the cleaning yourself or employ a cleaner? Or could you hire a cleaner for an hour or two a week to help you out, particularly if you joined up with a neighbour to make it worth your cleaner's while to come your way? Could you ask your family and friends to take their shoes off at the door to help to keep your floors clean? If you kept a supply of assorted slippers for guests? Is convenience food genuinely convenient? How convenient are frequently ill or ill-behaved children? Is driving always the fastest way to get somewhere, given parking problems on the one hand and more direct routes for pedestrians and cyclists on the other? (I and our two youngest on my bike regularly beat a neighbour in her car to playgroup.) Do you need the gym to exercise or could you stay fit (and save money) by cleaning house, cycling to the shops, and walking the children to school? There is a rut out there, a sea of assumptions, and – unless you find it suits you perfectly – there is absolutely no need to get into it.

Reintegrating. Divorcing home making from childcare hinges on funds to pay others to look after your home or else on devoting your windows of childfree time in the home to scrubbing toilets etc., which would make me, for one, rather resent my chores. Most mothers, past and present, have integrated home making with childcare, an approach that has several advantages. For one, it helps to teach children that their mother is not at their beck and call as she has work to do. Given the chance, children learn to cope with this just fine and go on to develop a most useful degree of self-sufficiency, provided, of course, the mother does regularly take time to be with them. Seeing their own mother getting her hands dirty and helping with the chores themselves, moreover, teaches children not to take meals, tidiness, and cleanliness for granted; they will begin to think twice about adding to the workload. It further helps children to understand home making as a family project and reduces their dependence on others.

And then there are the wider learning opportunities proffered by housework. The household is the "sensory theatre with sound, visual and tactile effects, vibration, aromas and music" par excellence.[10] In the household children can develop physically, mentally, and artistically, learn about machines and weights and measures, and ask their questions and assess your answers in the context of relevant activities ("what is this for?" "watch!") as they gain useful skills into the bargain. Working together, moreover, is a bonding experience: while you and your children shop, cook, bake, wash up, clean, and tidy up together you get to know each other better which helps to enhance your relationship and therefore also your children's emotional development. Difficult subjects, moreover, are often best broached with older children while working together. Finally, as your children observe your interaction with others in the course of your work in the home – with the neighbour who has just had a baby, the joiner who shares his life story, the cashier who recently immigrated, the builder who is renovating a house in France, the charity worker collecting for Christian Aid – they learn invaluable lessons about the world which no artificial learning environment can teach anywhere near as effectively.

Reskilling. A lot of people out there want to have a say in how we run our homes, what we buy, use, save, discard, how, where, and why we do one thing or another, or they want to do it for us. There is money in the practical aspect of mothering, so everybody wants a finger in the pie and the stakes are high. Your best response to the flood of information, disinformation, and solicitation coming at you is to reskill. Reskilling enables you to sort the sense from the nonsense. Reskilling, moreover, makes home making more enjoyable because it allows you to take charge of what you are doing and to challenge your intelligence and creativity as you acquire important knowledge and develop useful skills. Over my years of mothering, I have, for example, learned a lot about nutrition and now can assess the nutritional benefits of different foods, prepare nutritious meals, and even combat illness with food. As a result, I am not a victim of advertisers' jargon, take pride and pleasure in my knowledge and my skills, and know that my family benefits.[11] I can make tofu delicious, tomato sauce extremely nourishing, and quiche crust wholesome, I bake my own rye and spelt sourdough bread (low gluten), start the family off every weekday morning on a health-boosting smoothie, whiz up soups our toddlers love, make scones, chocolate ice-cream, as well as the occasional yummy, almost-good-for-you carrot cake, and, after a long search, have discovered the best chocolate cake... Above all, however, I am chuffed with my ability to use up every inch of vegetable from the weekly box scheme and to create a decent dinner with whatever is left in the fridge the night before the next delivery.

Popping a store-bought, so-called low fat pizza into the microwave is a dull job and cannot be other than dull. Cooking, on the other hand, is dull only to the ignorant and unskilled. To the knowledgeable and skilled, it is a creative act calling on in-depth knowledge as well as finely honed techniques developed over years of working creatively in the kitchen. Every meal is an accomplishment as well as an opportunity to increase your knowledge and skills. Home making skills further include time management, budgeting, interior design, the vast body of knowledge and skills associated with home remedies for minor ailments, the science of stain removal[12], the designing and making of fancy dress children's clothes, baking, birthday cake shaping and decorating[13], the art of flower arranging, cleaning[14], mending, and, my favourite, figuring out where to place furniture in your home so as to maximise space, comfort, and aesthetic pleasure. Home making is a skilled enterprise. Don't let the purveyors of quick-fix junk and ersatz wholesomeness convince you otherwise!

Resignifying. How, where, and why we do one thing or another, what we buy, use, save, discard, how we run our homes or let them be run by others has an impact on the world at large. Your routines have repercussions on economies as well as environments and therefore on the lives of millions of people. That alone makes home making significant. Will you shop from independent local traders to cut food miles or at the nearest hypermarket to cut costs? Will you buy fair trade bananas and forgo the box of chocolates to help others or buy cheap bananas as well as chocolates and help yourself? Will you buy eggs and meat from animals that had a life or buy eggs and meat from animals that didn't? Will you buy organic produce and ecologically sound cleaning products to protect the environment[15] or conventionally farmed produce and ecologically unsound cleaning products to protect your pocket? Will you buy yoghurt in large tubs and halve your bill or give in to your children's penchant for puddings in portion-sized plastic and double your rubbish? Will you make smoothies, sandwiches, soups, salads, and main meals from scratch and give your family fresh vitamins or get everything ready-made and give the world more packaging waste? Will you use bags and boxes to recycle paper, glass, cans, tins, and plastic bottles or throw it all in the same bin and be done? Will you use energy-saving light bulbs and save energy as well as money in the long term or buy conventional light bulbs and save money in the short term? Will you use cloth nappies and face the mess yourself or use disposables and pass it on?[16] Will you leave ten minutes earlier and walk and avoid polluting or quickly tidy up the kitchen and drive and avoid a spot of rain? Will you offer lifts to friends and neighbours whenever you do take the car to school or the shops or take the car whenever on your own because you cannot be bothered to offer lifts? Will you use the washing line outside and the clothes airer over the bath and save a lot of energy or use the tumble dryer and save a little labour? Will you try to put your time and money where your values are or put this book in the charity bag?[17] Decisions, decisions. There really is nothing trivial about home making once you think about it. All the more reason for us to give some thought to the principles which inform our practice.[18]

Closer to home, there is still more significance to be uncovered. Your approach to food selection and meal preparation influence your children's attitude to food and therefore their behaviour and performance at school as well as their present and future health. Schools certainly should do their bit to improve and maintain children's health by means of the food they serve, but if children come home to chicken nuggets and chips, crisps and chocolate bars, fizzy drinks and the television running[19], the schools' efforts will not bring about much overall improvement.[20] If most mothers bought organic, locally grown produce, cooked their own meals, and ate with their children at a table while engaging with them in background-noise-free conversation, on the other hand, the health of the nation, the environment, our local economies, and, last not least, our children would benefit enormously. It would take mothers time, time well spent. Perhaps the government would like to sponsor mothers who choose to spend their time in such broadly beneficial pursuits? We have had childcare vouchers in the UK to help us and our children to get out of the home, now we would like vegetable vouchers to be exchanged for vegetables from local suppliers to help us and our children to stay in the home, and healthy, too.[21]

Finally, home making significantly shapes our family life. Feast days, for example, whether Christmas and Easter, children's birthdays, other celebrations, or simply Sundays, become more meaningful and memorable to all participants when marked by knowledgeable, skilled, and shared home making activities such as decorating the home, baking, cooking, and extending hospitality to friends and family rather than merely by spending money on already prepared food, drink, venues, and entertainment. A well-loved home is, moreover and more generally, the centre of family life. It is the beginning and the end of our day, of our life, and of our striving. It is our foundation as well as our aspiration. It is the cradle as well as an expression of our personalities. It is a place of respite and a fount of well being. It is a comforting backdrop and a source of pleasure and pride. It is where we have space to pray as well as room to party. Home making is perhaps best understood as the enhancement of family life. We look after our home so that our home can look after us. Home making is intimately linked to everything else we do as mothers; it helps to support as well as to express our believing, loving, and forgiving. Home making therefore is a worthwhile activity, and it is worth our while putting our heart into it.

Managing people

Now that you are in control of things and, moreover, happy to be so, let us turn to the management of people by getting one thing straight straightaway: you are in charge, and it is in the interest of your husband as well as your children to support and bless your leadership. You, after all, have the experience and expertise in the home and know the requirements of the household. In addition, you know your family and are probably the only one with an overview of everyone's comings and goings.[22] Besides, you cannot run a home democratically; you would never get anything done (and, believe me, I have seen people try and they didn't). But this does not mean you have to be a despot about it, either. Think benign dictatorship, the only efficient form of government as long as there isn't a fool at the helm – and if you have persevered with mothering this far you are definitely no fool. Limit debate to issues other than home management but do allow everyone time and space to develop their own experience and expertise, and invite feedback. Think clear expectations and a mind receptive to sound advice and new perspectives.

The foundation is there. You have believed as well as loved and forgiven your children. You have shared your time and your values with them. You have got to know them. Now you want to get them to do things. You want them to take on responsibility for themselves as well as, eventually, for others. The obvious way to go about this is by delegating responsibility. Delegating responsibility is a multi-functional device. It is the only way to get something done without doing it. It is also the only way to render your children house-competent, and your children's house-competency is a great boon to themselves, to you, as well as to anyone else who will ever live with them.[23] You could think of delegating responsibility as an advanced kind of potty training: it is a hassle at first as you struggle to teach your children to remember and perform basic tasks but once they have learned them, life is a lot easier for all of you – and you will feel much better about sending your children into the world knowing that they master these skills. Children, moreover, thrive on being given responsibilities they can handle; they thrive on discovering their ever increasing abilities and they thrive on contributing positively to what matters to them most: their family life. Having important responsibilities in the home helps children to feel valued and to develop self-confidence. Delegating responsibility to children is furthermore a matter of *enabling* children. Children who can look after their teeth and their rooms, take care of their homework as well as their siblings, cook and wash up, plan their spare time and get themselves from A to B are children who have been enabled.[24]

Delegating responsibility also provides you with fantastic learning opportunities. My husband, for example, who was already supremely house-competent when I met him, cooks several evenings a week and has taught me over the years to pay as much attention to the flavour of the food as to its quantity and nutritional value... Our older children, moreover, regularly look after our younger children and never fail to come up with wonderfully inventive ways of playing with and teaching the little ones, some of which I learn to adopt. Delegating responsibility further offers you the opportunity to learn to keep your mouth shut for, sometimes, your learning curve refuses to budge and your only option is to stand back and appreciate the fact that we all do things differently. I am, for instance, familiar with two methods of tidying up a room covered in toys. The first method is my method. You put all the Lego into the

Lego bucket, Noah and Mrs Noah and the animals into the ark, the engines and tracks into the designated train-set box and the cars into the car box, then you find the missing jigsaw pieces and complete the jigsaws, sort the books back onto their size-specific shelves in the bookcase, hang up the dolls' dresses in the dolls' wardrobe, and put the dolls into their respective beds, making sure they have a pillow and a duvet each. The second method is my husband's method. You shove all the toys that are lying about into a pile under the cabin bed. And you are done. Now I can't, for the life of me, approve of my husband's method of tidying up. Sometimes I wish I could, as his method would save me time, time I could use to write poetry. And it's not as though our toddlers ever complain when they cannot find a toy; they simply play with something else. I cannot, however, see eye to eye with my husband on the subject of tidying up. But I'd be a fool to complain.

Delegating works best when the chores delegated match the sense, skills, and schedules of those to whom they are delegated. Our toddlers can clear their cups and plates, for example, but cannot quite yet set the table. And, yes, our older children excel at baby-sitting but are less than keen and therefore less than brilliant at it if I ask them to help out as soon as they come home from school. Offer a choice of duties, be open to feedback, and experiment with different distributions of duties until you find a pattern that suits everyone, and then redistribute duties as your children grow older. While your children should have a go at as many jobs in the home as possible, you will probably find that a fairly high degree of specialisation works best between you and your husband. Neither you nor your husband are still apprentices; concentrating on what you are good at, rather than dividing all tasks equally, is therefore probably the most sensible and efficient way to proceed. Delegating works best, moreover, if it is not erratic. If your children know what is expected of them, they can prepare themselves and will not feel as though you are constantly interfering with them. A routine also means that you do not have to reinvent the wheel every day and that your children learn to perform their chores as a matter of course, which is what you want. Make clear what needs doing but leave as much leeway regarding the how and when as possible and, of course, be flexible enough to make exceptions when necessary. I recently posted a chart with our older children's more onerous duties (the less onerous ones, such as switching off lights and cleaning teeth, I can take for granted). A nod in its direction now generally suffices as a reminder. A chart or rota, furthermore, lends an additional layer of authority: it is not only me who expects our son to set the table, IT SAYS SO ON THE CHART.

Moaning is tiresome, as is nagging – don't tolerate the former and try not to succumb to the latter. Talk through the reasons why certain jobs have to be done and do, by all means, include your own needs among those reasons. The 'yes... yes... and' method is a good one to use to communicate reasons; you ask two or three questions which you know your children will answer with a 'yes' so as to ensure that they are listening and to get your meaning across.[25] Work together with your children for a while when you introduce them to new chores and make jobs fun, if possible: set a timer for ten minutes and see how much tidying up you all can do in that period; put on music and sing with your children as you wash and dry dishes together. Make use of the fact that quite a few jobs are effectively treats for your children as children enjoy being given responsibility they can handle (and being left alone to get on with it) and enjoy seeing others appreciate the fruits of their labour. Small children will, for example, like sweeping up crumbs with a dustpan and brush and making their own pudding from plain yoghurt, maple syrup, and slices of banana and teenagers will almost certainly embrace the opportunity to plan and cook an entire meal for their family. Be as encouraging as you can as your children develop their skills and as appreciative as possible of the results. Focus – and help your children to focus – on what they can already do well, and notice small improvements. Praise specifically what worked (and try to ignore what didn't) as praise from you is your children's greatest motivator.[26] Let your children know that you consider them capable and responsible.

When you do need to remind your children of their duties, try to offer a choice; "you can sit down and stop splashing and stay in the bath or come out now", "you can practise your piano today for fifteen minutes or tomorrow for half an hour". Offering a choice helps to involve your children in decisions relevant to their lives and therefore helps to increase their sense of responsibility. Do not let your children lead you into a discussion on the why and wherefore of it all to get out of a job, instead resort to the broken record method which involves calmly repeating the choice you have decided to offer. If they fail to do their duty, make sure your children face the consequences. Now, the trick is to have consequences up your sleeve which are directly relevant to the duties in which your children have failed. If, for example, our toddlers do not help me to tidy-up their room, I only have time to read one story, not two; if they fight about a toy, I put the toy away; if our twelve-year-old daughter leaves her clothes on her bedroom floor, her clothes don't get washed; if our ten-year-old son doesn't get himself ready for school in time, he is late. Learning through consequences teaches children the point and purpose of their duties. It also prevents you and your children from ending up on opposing sides. Ideally, all concerned realise that it is at least as much in your children's interest as it is in your interest that your children learn to take on responsibility for themselves as well as, by and by, for others.

Awareness of potential pitfalls helps delegating to go more smoothly. Question your assumptions before laying down the law. If, for example, you insist that your toddler puts away one toy before getting out another, you effectively

136

restrict her creativity as mixing toys often is part of imaginative play. Also, does a teenager's bedroom need to be tidy at all times or is that asking too much? Don't expect your children to take on duties which they cannot yet manage; do, on the other hand, regularly review your routine to see whether your children are ready for new responsibilities. Ensure that you have made your expectations clear and have been heard – eye contact helps. What is obvious to you is not necessarily obvious to your children! Give your children the time and space to learn at their own pace and to develop their own methods; this will often involve giving them the opportunity to make a mess![27] Don't underrate the importance of transitions. Your children confront different sets of expectations in different environments and need time to adjust from one to the other. Walking to and from school rather than driving, for instance, allows your children a helpful period of transition. A ten-minute warning before you need your children's help also gives them time to wind up what they are doing and to prepare themselves inwardly for a change of pace. If you have several children of similar age, the question of fairness will inevitably come up. It is most easily resolved by leaving the detail of the distribution of duties to your children along the 'one cuts the cake, the other picks the first piece' principle. As with all squabbling, children are generally very good at sorting it out themselves when left to it and you should only interfere if there is physical danger (e.g., in the kitchen) or bullying. Pick your fights.

Not all duties are equally important; concentrate on those that matter most and leave the others for later. Try to be consistent. If your approach is haphazard or receptive to wheedling, your children will fail to take their duties seriously. Do not routinely offer rewards for duties done. The goal is to teach your children to develop skills and act responsibly, not to turn them into mercenaries. Prevent your role from being reduced to that of grand-inquisitor by listening to and talking with your children as well as joining in activities with your children which all enjoy. Remember, in other words, to be there for them. Finally, deflate tension by laughing together. Children can be incredibly funny, especially if you are a willing subject of their humour. Laughing about yourself won't detract from your authority: simply wipe away your tears of laughter after a while and insist on the point behind whatever inspired their parody.

When delegating responsibility to your children works, it works because you have shared your time and your values as well as your chores with your children. Delegating responsibility to your children, in turn, is an effective way of sharing your time and values with your children! Take food, for example. Children can join in family meals and eat family food from their first birthday, if not before. Good food becomes much more interesting when it is shared with others and, moreover, seen to be enjoyed by others. And good table manners make much more sense if you are not the only one eating and also have the chance to observe others' good example. As they grow older, your children can increasingly help in the kitchen with preparing food and clearing up. An understanding of these processes will further increase their appreciation of good food as well as their consideration for those who provide it.

Similarly, your children's approach to television, computer games, and the internet hinges on your input, or lack of it. Television and computers prevent children from doing what children need to be doing: moving, exploring, thinking, creating, sharing, communicating, questioning.[28] As a result, children come away from the screen tenser. They also lose the ability to entertain themselves. Chances are, therefore, that they will get on your nerves and you, too, will be less rather than more relaxed – as well as tempted to send them straight back to the screen! Long-term, moreover, you are in for a diversion of values between you and your children as your children learn about the world from the two-dimensional entertainment presented to them on screen rather than from your example and conversation. Internet chatting similarly prevents children from doing much of what they need to be doing in order to develop as interaction via the internet does not involve much in the way of sharing, observing, and looking after and therefore severely limits what children learn about relationships. If, on the other hand, you make a point of regularly relaxing *with* your children – eating with them, listening to them, playing with them, talking to them, going to the park with them – both you and your children will not only be more relaxed but also grow closer. Your children, moreover, will remain able to occupy themselves by themselves without the help of gadgets[29] and to interact with others in person – as well as motivated to stick to highly restricted screen times.[30]

When delegating responsibility to your children works, it really works. Your children develop good, responsible habits and your life in the home is a great deal easier: you are not hassled by your duties nor do you have to hassle your children about theirs. Your children, moreover, can enjoy greater freedom. You have no need to pen in your children with excessive academic pressure and a non-stop extracurricular programme to ensure that they spend their time sensibly. Because you have taught your children to act responsibly, you can trust them to make sound decisions and to look after themselves as well as others. This means that you do not have to worry (much) when they are off, doing their own thing, which is just as well as doing their own thing is what your children will increasingly want to do. In giving your children responsibilities you have given them structure, and structure – as we have seen already several times in this book – is not something which constrains but something which *supports* and therefore frees, both them and you.

139

Managing

Are we managing? Of course we are managing! And how we are managing! Is there anything we are not managing? Time, space, activity, rest, input, output, wants, needs, money, things, children, plumbers, dogs, hamsters, furniture, food – you name it, we are managing it. We are, after all, home managers. But are we managing *all right*? Now, that is a different question.

Inspired by a devout friend, I once stuck a little note to myself on the fridge: *YOU WILL NEVER REGRET HAVING GIVEN.* After some weeks, however, I added in the margin: *except when I get completely exhausted and then become extremely irritable.* Yes, sometimes I lose it. And that hermit's cave on a mountaintop, not the kitchen amid my family, is where I want to be. And I wonder how I will go on, as I must go on.

To judge from articles in women's magazines, perseverance comes from the tub. A long soak in the bath tub and – having enjoyed the pleasures of hot water, bath oils, bath pearls, perfumed candles, champagne, hair treatments, and face masks – the worn-out woman re-emerges full of vigour and optimism. I am not convinced, however. In fact, I am certain that there are more effective ways of managing to persevere. Here are some.

Be prepared. An education is never wasted on a mother as a mother passes her education on to her children through her mothering. An education, however, also helps a mother to persevere in her mothering. It was not until I nursed our firstborn, for hours, every day, for months, that I understood the true value of my studies and travels. I would sit there, hands full of baby, and a head full of reflections. I doubt I would have coped without the richness of experience to draw on.

Get sleep. I could sing an ode to sleep, if I could sing. Much of the world has the excellent custom of an afternoon siesta. I started my own siesta habit after the birth of our third child when I was no longer as young as I used to be and could not keep going without stopping after a bad night. So I cuddled up to our baby to make sure that he would not disturb me and slept every afternoon for at least twenty minutes, and I have been sleeping in the afternoons ever since. Our third child is not a baby anymore and allowed to watch a video after I have put his younger sister into the cot for her nap. I also turn the telephone off and stick a note to the front door with blue tack: PLEASE DO NOT KNOCK OR RING DOORBELL AS BABY IS ASLEEP. Never mind the fact that our youngest would not actually be disturbed by a knock or the doorbell – it is I who need the break. After my rest, I feel refreshed and ready to face the second half of the day. Whenever I am not breastfeeding, moreover, we have also managed to enjoy lie-ins on Saturdays by permitting our children to watch television on Saturday mornings (and only on Saturday mornings!). They get themselves up and tiptoe downstairs, keen not to disturb my husband and me lest we disturb them with breakfast preparations.

Eat well. You need decent sources of energy to maintain your output. In addition to healthy meals based on fresh fruit and vegetables, whole grains and pulses, nuts and seed, consider adding wholesome snacks. Apricot kernel butter[31] sandwiches filled with a sliced banana and several mugs of green or black tea do it for me.

Get help. It is wise to know your limits and stop and ask for help before you reach them. Your husband and parents as well as parents-in-law are obvious ports of call. You could furthermore swap childcare with a friend who has children or find a kind neighbour who enjoys children and is willing to help out once in a while in exchange for lifts to the shops, perhaps. If you can afford it, hire a cleaner for a couple of hours a week while you are mothering a baby.

Mix. Especially if you are a first time mother, meeting up with other mothers is important to overcome isolation and find out how others are managing. It also gives your children a chance to mix. Church, parent and toddler groups, and parks are good places to meet other mothers. Meeting up with friends who are not mothers can be stimulating or frustrating in the early days of motherhood depending on the tolerance you have for each others' very different lives.

Exercise. Of course, cleaning house, walking to school, and cycling to the shops gives you plenty of exercise. For the sake of persevering with it all, however, additional exercise may be called for. Swimming, yoga, power walking, and, most recently, street dancing all have helped me at different times to persevere in my mothering because they have stretched parts of me that mothering does not challenge – yoga, in particular, does that – and because they have been fun.

Work. As though you didn't have enough of it! But, seriously, work, whether paid or not, besides your mothering can help you to structure your day and get more out of it once the initial shocks of motherhood have subsided. Only, do not allow other projects to take over; mothering is more important. In the past, I have enjoyed working part-time outside the home while being a mother and lately I have enjoyed writing this book while staying at home full-time. I leave articles I should read lying around to pick up when I have a minute. In addition, I have made up a 'cosy corner' with an old cot mattress, a rug, and a few toys and books in the room where I work so that the little ones can play alongside me when I write; a friend put a small chair and table with paper and crayons into her study and her youngest has become an intent artist as a result. Although I am largely preoccupied with our four children and home making, I manage to find time to sit at my desk because I look forward to the pleasure of writing, and because I have a deadline.

Use the duller tasks of mothering. These tasks are like swimming fifty lengths, like practising scales, like knitting a scarf. Unless I am listening to the radio or chatting with the children, these jobs allow my mind to focus on something else[32], to wander freely, or else to empty itself. And then, after that delicious mental respite, I even have something to show for it: a clean home, ironed shirts, gleaming shoes. I usually look forward to washing-up in the evenings, for example. The children are fed and generally happy at this point and are busy playing, reading, or practising their instruments. And as my hands work, efficiently cleaning dishes with as little water as possible, as you know (and there is satisfaction in that), I enjoy my solitude and let my mind go wherever it takes me, which is sometimes nowhere at all. Yes, you can think at the sink – and find meditative bliss there, too.

Sing. Singing and work go well together. I really enjoy going out into the garden at dusk, for example, to sing as I take down and fold the washing. I hope the neighbourhood enjoys it, too. If you sing as you work, you can consciously decide what the backing vocals, so to speak, of your home-making are. Clearly, something joyful is a good idea. Eva Cassidy's

Since love is Lord of Heaven and Earth,
how can I keep from singing?

always cheers me.

Appreciate the authenticity of your vocation. Your work as a mother anchors you in a fundamental sanity and in the present.[33] Through mothering, you are generally meeting genuine needs rather than contributing to the elaboration of artificial wants. Your routines as well as the inevitable interruptions, moreover, constantly recall you to what matters, here and now. And the here and now is, of course, the only reality you got.

Be philosophical. Most troubles pass. Dirt and disastrous dinners, certainly, are nothing to worry about for long, if at all. Take a deep breath, gain perspective, clear up. The American Buddhist teacher and mother, Yvonne Rand, found that a practice called the half-smile made a big difference to her body and mind. You lift the corners of

143

your mouth slightly and hold them there for three breaths. The half-smile when practised six or more times a day can help you to understand obstacles as teachers and to develop patience.[34] I should practise it.

Use the soft no. When your child hassles you, the child psychologist Steve Biddulph recommends that you relax your shoulders and your entire body, smile inwardly, and say "no" very softly, as often as necessary until the temptation to yell passes (or your child gives up).[35]

Use consequences. We have already seen that using consequences is very educational for your children. Using consequences is, however, also very therapeutic for you. When I confront a tip in our eldest daughter's bedroom these days, for instance, I no longer boil and rage and demand instant rectification, I simply move on with the vacuum cleaner and think, "Great, I won't have to clean her room." Very therapeutic indeed.

Take time out. You don't have to go far. My best times out are Friday and Saturday evenings in. The children eat a simple supper I make from leftovers I kept in the freezer. My husband then puts the little ones to bed with some help from the big ones and cooks our dinner. I have a shower and come down to wine and olives, the table set with candles, Nina Simone singing about life and love, and the aroma of chillies wafting through the kitchen. I love the table setting and the music, the food and the company.[36] And I love not being in charge for a bit. If you like the idea but your husband cannot or will not cook, see whether he is happy to boil fresh pasta and open a jar of pesto. It'll take him five minutes and, who knows, he may discover a passion.

Be grateful. Take time, every day, to concentrate on feeling grateful! Thank God for your children, your home, your husband, your husband's mothering… and for the joys of the moment such as your children's most recent antics and accomplishments, the good food on the table, the caress from your husband in passing. Know that you are blessed – and make a point of counting your blessings.

Pray. The best so-called 'me-time', I have found, is He-time. What better place to go when you are weary and heavy laden than to Him who promised to give you rest?![37] The contemplative practice of prayer helps to sustain the everything-but contemplative practice of mothering; in prayer, we encounter God and receive from Him so that we may give: "[…] time devoted to God in prayer not only does not detract from effective and loving service to our neighbour but is in fact the inexhaustible source of that service".[38] As a mother, you are never short of reasons to pray. You may want to ask for strength, help, and guidance for yourself, your husband, or your children in specific situations, to express gratitude, to pray for those who suffer, and to pray for the world your children will inherit. And there are many ways, times, and places to pray. I thank God for the day in the mornings, acknowledge worries with silent Hail Mary's throughout the day, say grace with everyone else at the table in the evenings[39], and sing a prayer with the little ones and sometimes pray with the big ones about particular concerns at bedtime. I usually pray while breastfeeding, moreover, and always after taking Holy Communion. And I love Exposition. During Exposition, the Blessed Sacrament is exposed on the altar and people adore it, silently recite prayers or pray in their own words, or simply sit in His presence. In daylight, the Blessed Sacrament, despite the splendour of the monstrance in which it is placed and the candles beside it, is barely discernible among the many images in the church. But there it is, God made flesh to dwell among us, made humble food to feed us. I sit or kneel in front of it and know that God is always there, waiting with infinite patience for me to find Him. At night, in an otherwise dimly lit church, the Blessed Sacrament appears to shine forth from the altar, drawing eyes to it. I sit or kneel in front of it and know that God's light touches me also. I usually stay for about twenty minutes, then re-enter the current of my day.

Keep presence of God. When we are interrupted, yet again, annoyed, or tired, it helps to recall God's persevering presence in the Blessed Sacrament as humanity goes about its business of interrupting, annoying, tiring. God is always there, always ready to love. He does not stomp off and slam doors behind him. He does not give up. There is no stomping off, no slamming of doors, there is no giving up for mothers either. As mothers, we are called to remain, and to remain ready to love in all circumstances. Remaining close to God in and through prayer enables us to do so.

Put love into it. Every act, however humble, can communicate love or be offered up for loved-ones and their needs. St Josemaria Escriva advised those who would be thorough-going Christians to carry out the minutest detail of their daily duties with love of God.[40] Like Jesus, we are called to serve our God and our neighbour. And it is through conscientious and loving service that we become more like Christ and contribute to our sanctification. Our chores are, in effect, "the raw material of [our] holiness".[41] St Thérèse of Lisieux particularly excelled at practising love and abdication of self will in what de Caussade called the "sacrament of the present moment".[42] Jesus washed his disciples' feet the night before he died. I'll probably be cleaning the loo.

Have faith. When problems trouble you, remind yourself that you do not have the big picture. But God does. And, in time, He will reveal it to you if you remain receptive to His Word through prayer, patience, and humility. Try to maintain stability of soul in the face of success as well as failure. You are not all-knowing and all-controlling, and your children are not your own. Your life and your children's lives are gifts from God. Do your best, let God take care of the rest.

Bear your cross. The value of suffering is the profoundest Christian mystery. And, being a mystery, it is anything but obvious. If you have a heavy cross to bear, take comfort and courage from the fact that Jesus is at your side, ready to carry you as you carry your cross. Also, take comfort and courage from the fact that he has gone before you. Jesus did not want to suffer. He sweated blood in agony in the Garden of Gethsemane. But then he accepted his suffering. He endured taunts and torture without rage or self-pity. He showed us the virtue and strength that lie at the core of suffering patiently born. And through his Resurrection, he has suffused our darkest hour with the light of hope.

When we accept our suffering, we can grow deeper and come to love more deeply; we can transform trials into lessons which help us to grow closer to God, to develop fortitude and enlarge our capacity to forgive. The process is painful but precious. In our helplessness, we abandon ourselves entirely to God. We cry out to Him for help and trust that His loving will be done, remembering that if we understand Him, He is not God.[43] When we suffer, it is especially difficult but also especially important to keep up our Christian practices: to keep praying, seeking out the sacraments, reading spiritual texts, and to keep communicating God's love. The physicality of many Catholic devotional practices is of great benefit here: the acts of kneeling or standing at different points in the mass, the lighting of prayer candles, the fingering of beads while praying the rosary, the repetition of memorised prayers, even when there is turmoil within, help to recall us to God's love. It is obedience, now as so often before, that sustains and strengthens us. In time we will find that, like Jesus after the darkness of the tomb, we can rise again.

Hope. Supernatural hope, like faith and love, is a gift: we have to pray for it. In daily practice, however, hope, again like faith and love, is primarily an act of the will: we have to apply it; we have to live by it and base our actions on it by being patient and humble in all things.[44] Understanding our redemption provides a foundation for our hope. God has overcome evil. This is a fundamental fact of our faith which teaches us that we need not be afraid. It teaches us not to despair but to rely on God's guidance and to keep close to His love. It teaches us to hold out for the hidden flowering in times of sorrow. It teaches us to look hopefully for good in or beyond what appears entirely evil. It teaches us to see the resurrection in the cross. Supernatural hope draws us forward and upward. When we have received the gift of supernatural hope, we can look at the fickleness of worldly promise, at our failings, and at our fears, and say, with Julian of Norwich: in the end all will be well and every manner of being will be well.

Our hope for heaven in the hereafter helps us to strive for holiness in the here and now. Because there is a goal – a time and a place when we will see God face to face and see[45] – the battles we confront now are worth fighting, the pain we suffer now is worth enduring. Our supernatural hope gives meaning and direction to our struggles and sustains us: because we hope, we know that getting up tomorrow to love better, forgive more, and work harder is worthwhile. Because *God wants us*, it makes sense to keep wanting Him, to keep approaching His love by striving for holiness through what we do, here and now.

Endowed with supernatural hope, we can give hope to those around us. We can teach our children about the promise of eternal beatitude. We can teach them to avoid both presumption and despair by continually seeking and trusting God's loving guidance. We can teach them that "reality is gracious, forgiving, redeeming and absolutely trustworthy".[46] Our children, like us, will then live endowed with a central core of light that shines in the darkness, and keeps shining. They will be courageous. They will know joy. And they will persevere.

NOTES

1 William Morris's criteria.
2 Pardon this lengthy quotation, but do persevere with it! Commenting on modern consumer behaviour, the sociologist Anthony

Giddens writes in *Modernity and Identity,* (Cambridge: Polity, 1991) p. 198:

"To a greater or lesser degree, the project of the self becomes translated into one of the possession of desired goods and the pursuit of artificially framed styles of life. [...] The consumption of ever-novel goods becomes in some part a substitute for the genuine development of self; appearance replaces essence as the visible signs of successful consumption come actually to outweigh the use-values of the goods and services in question themselves. Bauman [Zygmunt Bauman, *Legislators and Interpreters,* (Cambridge: Polity, 1989): 189] expresses this well: 'Individual needs of personal autonomy, self-definition, authentic life or personal perfection are all translated into the need to possess, and consume, market-offered goods. This translation, however, pertains to the appearance of use value of such goods, rather than to the use value itself; as such, it is intrinsically inadequate and ultimately self-defeating, leading to momentary assuagement of desires and lasting frustration of needs...The gap between human needs and individual desires is produced by market domination; this gap is, at the same time, a condition of its reproduction. The market feeds on the unhappiness it generates: the fears, anxieties and the sufferings of personal inadequacy it induces release the consumer behaviour indispensable to its continuation.'"

3 Karen Kingston, *Clear your Clutter with Feng Shui* (London: Piatkus, 1998) p. 113.

4 In proposing this procedure I am assuming that your husband and children are both useful and beautiful.

5 Oxfam and the British Red Cross will take your mobile phones; Vision Aid Overseas and Help the Aged will redistribute your spectacles; contact www.computeraid.org.international to recycle your computer and www.icer.org.uk to recycle electronic equipment. The Furniture Reuse Network (www.frn.org.uk) will recycle your washing machine or fridge.

6 One idea is to collect not-so-beautiful and not-so-useful sentimental items such as a *selection* of children's paintings, letters, diaries, and such in a 'memory box'. I use large boxes with lids designed to fit under beds.

7 Luckily for our children, a bit of dirt is good for you: the more hygienic a household, the greater the likelihood children living in it will develop asthma or eczema, *Archives of Disease in Childhood,* 2002: 87, p. 269.

8 For further information on cloth nappies, see www.realnappy.com

9 *Moltex* nappies, made in Germany, see www.moltex.de or moltex.info@ontexglobal.com

10 This quotation is for real. It is taken from a description of a childcare centre in south Manchester.

11 The downside of all this is, of course, that it is immensely frustrating when I feel like eating junk and cannot find a single unhealthy item of food in the house.

12 The best advice I have ever received on treating stains was this: "Simply imagine it only just happened." Nobody can expect you to remove fresh stains straightaway, so you can relax about them. Well, I can.

13 My most recent effort: a huge hairy spider.

14 Absolutely. Cleaning requires knowledge and skills, and therefore training. The fact that cleaning companies generally do not train their staff is astounding, and a reflection of widespread ignorance about home making.

15 Another big plus, in case you need more convincing, of organic produce and ecologically sound products is that choosing exclusively these radically reduces choice which renders shopping much simpler. Who wants to gauge the relative worth of ten types of loo roll, twenty brands of washing-up liquid, and fifty different breakfast cereals?

16 For every one pound spent on disposables in the UK it costs the taxpayer ten pence to dispose of them. It takes one of these nappies 500 years to break down. Compared to cloth nappies, disposables use 3.5 times the energy, 2.3 times the waste water, 8.3 times the raw non-renewable material, and up to 30 times the land for growing raw materials (source: www.unicorn-grocery.co.uk).

17 In other words: I know I am annoying.

18 To help you consider, you could read *Shopped*, by Joanna Blythman, *Fast Food Nation*, by Eric Schlosser, *Not on the Label*, by Felicity Lawrence, and *The Good Shopping Guide*, published by Ethical Marketing Group. You could also contact:
the Fairtrade Foundation (www.fairtrade.org.uk),
the Ethical Consumer (www.ethicalconsumer.org),
the Women's Environmental Network (www.wen.org.uk),
the Good Food Foundation (goodfood@xs4all.nl), and
EcoTeams in your area (www.globalactionplan.org.uk and look at the following websites: www.greenprices.com,
www.saveenergy.co.uk and chooseclimate.org).
In addition to these and other excellent initiatives, it is high time that the government require the impact of consumer items on human welfare, animal welfare, and the environment to be clearly indicated on the product, for example by means of a points system.

19 What is it with all these television cooks? Is the idea that they are cooking – publicly and proficiently – so that the rest of us don't

have to? A *third* of the average UK spending on food goes on convenience food (Mintel, Dieting January 2006).

20 School meals provide only about 17 per cent of pupils' annual intake of food, *Manchester People* (the newspaper of Manchester City Council), No 28, Autumn 2006.

21 The government can finance vegetable vouchers by increasing the tax on sugary foods, crisps, and ready-meals and through long-term savings in the health sector.

22 Especially if you keep a family calendar, that is, a calendar with a space each day for each member of your family.

23 A recent survey by the British Heart Foundation of eight to 15-year-olds found that, while 99 per cent of children can use a DVD player; fewer than half can boil an egg, *Manchester Metro News*, 29 September 2006. Bad news.

24 The child psychologist Steve Biddulph offers a valuable, counter-cultural perspective on the theme of delegating responsibility to children: "A lot of kids [in the West] don't grow up (that is, they don't take responsibility for their own care and feeding) until they are in their early twenties. [...] All around the world, from Nepal to New Guinea to Nicaragua, it's normal for young children to have responsibilities. They are usually under watchful adult care, (not neglected like many affluent western children), but they have their daily round of chores, which they carry out quite cheerfully and with obvious pride. There is time for play, but this is incidental. The result of this working childhood is that in almost every other culture of the world, childhood flows smoothly and easily into adult life. How did we ever get the idea that childhood is a 'waiting room' before life begins?" Steve Biddulph, *The Secret of Happy Children,* (London: Thorsons, 1998) pp. 84-5.

25 Fernando Corominas, *Training the Will* (Madrid: Palabra). An example of this method would be: "Do you know why it is important to clean your teeth after a meal?" "Yes." "Do you remember how Tom had to have a filling because he didn't clean his teeth often enough?" "Yes." "And you don't want a filling, do you?"

26 Next Generation Coaching recommend a ratio of praise to criticism of at least 5:1! (www.nextgenerationcoaching.co.uk)

27 This is a key aspect of Maria Montessori's childrearing philosophy, see Maria Montessori, *The Secret of Childhood.*

28 Cf. Miriam Stoppard, *Test your Child,* (London: Dorling Kindersley, 1991) pp. 135-6.

29 On a good day, for instance, our twelve-year-old will bake a cake for the family, compose a song on the piano, and jog around the block three times. And our ten-year-old will develop a new smoothie recipe, practise shooting arrows in the garden, and improvise on

his electric guitar. All on their own initiative. (On a bad day, they will hang around and complain about being bored.)

30 I suggest an hour a day of material of which you approve. It is best to watch television *with* your children as they can then pick up on your perspective on the programmes. (This is, however, asking too much of me.)

31 It is not advisable to eat nut butters when you are breastfeeding if there is a history of allergies in your or your husband's family as it may trigger allergic reactions in your baby.

32 That is how I planned and revised much of this book.

33 Cf. Fr Ronald Rolheiser, 'In praise of ordinary lives that we despise', *The Catholic Herald*, 2 November 2001.

34 Vickie Mackenzie, *Cave in the Snow*, (London: Bloomsbury, 1998) p. 194.

35 Steve Biddulph, *The Secret of Happy Children*, (London: Thorsons, 1998) p. 121.

36 The special-evenings-together habit is, incidentally, a good one to get into for the sake of your marriage. It helps you to keep in touch, even in difficult times.

37 "Come to me, all who labour and are heavy laden, and I will give you rest." (Matthew 11:28)

38 Pope Benedict XVI, *Deus Caritas Est*, 36.

39 For the hand that feeds us, for the heart that loves us, for the grace that saves us, Lord we thank thee.

40 [now: Saint] Josemaria Escriva de Balaguer, *Friends of God*, (London: Scepter, 1981) p. 5.

41 Fr Peter Bristow, *Opus Dei: Christians in the Midst of the World*, (London: Catholic Truth Society, 2001) p. 48.

42 J.-P. de Caussade, *The Sacrament of the Present Moment*, (New York: Harper & Row, 1982).

43 "Si comprehendis, non est Deus – if you understand him, he is not God", St Augustine, *Sermo* 52, 16: PL 38, 360.

44 "Hope is practised through the virtue of patience, which continues to do good even in the face of apparent failure, and through the virtue of humility, which accepts God's mystery and trusts him even at times of darkness," Pope Benedict XVI, *Deus Caritas Est*, p. 39.

45 "For now we see in a mirror dimly, but then face to face." (1 Corinthians, 13:12)

46 Fr Ronald Rolheiser, *The Catholic Herald*, 17 August 2001.

6
hoping

Mothers are fierce hopers. When a mother thinks about being pregnant, she hopes that she has the faith, love, forgiveness, and perseverance needed to mother. When a mother thinks about giving birth, she hopes that she will cope with the initial pain and the ensuing strain. When a mother holds her baby, she hopes that her love and her care will ward off all ills that may come her baby's way. When a mother introduces the world to her child and her child to the world, she hopes that goodness and kindness will mark her child's path. When a mother returns home from work, she hopes that her teenager will have hung up the washing. There is much to hope for when you are a mother!

In this final chapter, I sum up my thoughts on mothering, give reasons for hope, and point to a bright future for mothers, children, and for society as a whole. I begin, however, by listing some sad facts. We do, after all, need to apply hope to the issues rather than use hope to avoid the issues. And many of the issues confronting mothers and children in particular and society in general are very sad indeed. I am, however, genuinely hopeful – which is remarkable given that I spent my childhood in a country where pessimism is considered a sure sign of intellectual vigour and now live in a time and in a place blindly bent, it seems, on destroying that which alone can give hope. But then again, it isn't remarkable at all: as a mother and a Christian, how can I be anything but hopeful?

Some sad facts: Leading childcare experts, among them Steve Biddulph and Penelope Leach, warn that babies and young children do not thrive in institutional settings.[1] One study, for example, indicates that babies and toddlers experience higher stress levels at nurseries than when cared for mainly by their mothers.[2] Research has shown, moreover, that children's emotional development and their ability to learn are closely intertwined and that a crucial period in a child's emotional development falls between the ages of six months and twenty months.[3] Nonetheless, more children are now cared for outside the home than in it and the number of childminders is decreasing whereas the number of nurseries is increasing in the UK. The number of school children with behavioural problems or learning difficulties is increasing as well. The trend towards extending school opening hours continues even though experts have cautioned that institution-based after-school care can adversely affect children's emotional health.[4] Both mothers and fathers are spending less and less time at home which has a detrimental effect on family life. Many children arrive at school too hungry to learn. Only a minority of children in the UK eat cooked meals in their homes, and most children determine what they eat themselves. Tooth decay and obesity are significant problems among children.

Excessive alcohol consumption is increasingly common among teenagers as well as among the general population, as are casual sex and sexually transmitted infections. The UK abortion rate continues to rise steadily despite the ready availability of contraceptives and morning-after pills. Marriage and birth rates are declining. Forty per cent of births occur outside marriage, and one in five children in Britain is now born into a home without a father.[5] Cohabitation is on the increase. Across every income group, cohabiting couples are at least twice as likely as married couples to end their relationship.[6] Surveys indicate that the number of people living alone and feeling lonely is increasing.

Given the above, I cannot but wonder whether someone has pressed our self-destruct button. Society is evidently in the process of disintegrating. More and more of its fragments are solitarily spinning in space, fundamentally alone, joining up here and there only now and again to binge drink, shop, or have sex, as well as to work because the things that maintain us in and distract us from our loneliness cost money. In the meantime, our superhero who could save us all – I am referring, of course, to *THE MOTHER* – is stuck in the phone booth. Isolated and unsupported in the home, her job belittled and beleaguered, she is perpetually engaged in an identity crisis. Financial and social pressures, moreover, are driving her into full-time employment and, frankly, she is no longer so sure she wants to spend any time with the demanding and irritating brats who are the children she did not bother to mother.

But, hey, let us not pass the buck! Let us not fall prey to popular disparaging portrayals of mothering intended to facilitate passing the buck. We know better. We know that mothering is incredibly rewarding work which gives us invaluable time with our children and incomparable autonomy. We know that mothering provides us with endless opportunities to expand our horizons as we confront a vast variety of challenges. We know that mothering is a highly complex undertaking requiring excellent management skills as well as the ability to acquire and apply all manner of knowledge. We know that mothering demands extraordinary emotional commitment and extreme perseverance. We know, moreover, that mothering is fantastically important work as it communicates beliefs, love, values, and a sense of responsibility to our children and therefore shapes the adults our children will become. Mothering contributes profoundly to the functioning of our homes, our communities, our society, and our economy. And we know that it takes mothers to mother.

So let us get out those capes, get out of the phone booths, and save society! I am hopeful that we can. All we need to do is to *integrate our mothering*, to take us and our children into account as whole persons when we mother, and to demand policies as well as facilities that help us to *integrate mothering into society*. And then, with capes flying, we can move society forward, from fragmentation to healing and wholeness.

Integrated mothering

Consider once more the breast, the symbol of the model of mothering introduced in the first chapter and referred to throughout this book. Mothering as represented by the breast involves the mother in her entirety, as a person with beliefs, emotions, and values, a body, and limited time and energy, and the child likewise as a spiritual, emotional, social, and physical being. The model of mothering symbolised by the breast understands mothering as consisting of different aspects which correspond to the different aspects or dimensions of a person. The model of mothering symbolised by the breast, moreover, recognises that the different aspects of mothering are inextricably intertwined and interdependent exactly as the different dimensions of a person are inseparable. The model of mothering symbolised by the breast furthermore points to the fact that every aspect of mothering contributes to the flourishing of life and love, which is what mothering is about. The model of mothering symbolised by the breast, finally, acknowledges the centrality of the spiritual dimension: it guides mothers to work from the centre outward and encourages us to take God as our model in our mothering, to follow His loving example.

In the model of mothering symbolised by the breast, the nipple symbolises believing. This is the spiritual aspect of mothering and is represented by the central circle of the model of mothering. Our faith provides us with a profound and necessary source of sustenance, guidance, and hope throughout our mothering. By trying to live in accordance with our beliefs, moreover, we discover the will of God for us and, if we persist, the joy of realising our full humanity. We learn that what God asks of us is not always easy. But we also learn that God is always there to sustain and guide us and to give us hope, and that God loves us.

When we come to grips with the spiritual aspect of mothering, we understand that our child is a gift – not a right, nor a mistake – and that we do well to embrace this gift. We experience, moreover, that obedience to the Word of Him-who-loves-us-best is better, for all concerned, than obedience to the noise emanating from the rest. We also cease to rely on our own wavering fortune, strength, and cleverness to muster confidence, and instead find fortitude in faith.

The areola symbolises loving. This is the emotional aspect of mothering and is represented by the second circle of the model of mothering. When we receive our baby, many of us are cut loose from what we know and thrown into the deep end of the unknown. As we struggle to the surface, we are terribly tired as well as frightfully uncertain as we become aware of our awesome responsibilities. Given time and support – time and support which allow us to be there for our baby – we learn to love our baby unconditionally. Our sense of self changes profoundly as we do so: we become mothers. In loving our baby unconditionally, we draw on God's unconditional love for us. And just as God's love for us helps us to grow as human beings, so our love for our baby, our being there for our baby, allows our baby to grow.

When we come to grips with the emotional aspect of mothering, we understand that we develop as mothers by being there for our baby – by being available, attentive, and responsive to our baby. We also understand that our baby's physical, emotional, mental, and spiritual development, in turn, depends on us communicating acceptance, respect, interest, and concern to our baby by being available, attentive, and responsive. We understand that love takes time and that love gives time, and that our children never stop needing our love. And we understand that it is our love, not our children's genetic make-up, which makes our children perfect.

The fleshy bulk of the breast symbolises forgiving. This is the social aspect of mothering and is represented by the third circle of the model of mothering. As human beings we depend on a moral framework to guide our interaction with others and find genuine self-fulfilment. We do well, therefore, to look to our Creator for guidance and to think long, hard, and often about the implications of our values for our behaviour and to remain keenly conscious of our fallibility. We frequently need to seek God's forgiveness to help us to improve our behaviour and remain in communion with Him. Similarly, we frequently need to seek our children's forgiveness in order to improve our mothering and remain in communion with them.

As Jesus taught us, so we have to teach our children. We have to share with our children our faith and impart to them a moral framework. And we need to show our children by means of our conversation and example the behavioural implications of that faith and moral framework. We need, moreover, to enrol others – above all our husbands, but also family, friends, neighbours, teachers, coaches, congregations, clubs, communities, the government, the media – in the task of the moral formation of our children. Like God, we must draw a distinction between the sinner and the sin and continue to love our children even when we cannot approve their actions. And, like God, we have to welcome our children back into our embrace when they have sinned and assist them in renewing their efforts for good.

When we come to grips with the social aspect of mothering, we never stop striving for holiness in ourselves and in our children. We understand that our responsibility as mothers is far greater than to please our children: our responsibility as mothers is to guide our children. We are, therefore, prepared for necessary conflict but are also ever ready to forgive. We understand that our children – like us – need values, need boundaries in which to find themselves, for else they will be lost.

The perimeter of the breast which connects the breast to the rest of the body symbolises persevering. This is the practical aspect of mothering and is represented by the outermost circle of the model of mothering. This aspect of mothering involves both managing things and managing people. There are many effective ways of rendering our management of things both easier and more meaningful and thereby more enjoyable. We manage our children primarily by delegating responsibility to them according to their competence. Delegating responsibility to our children allows our children to contribute to family life and feel appreciated, to develop new skills and therefore greater confidence, and to become house-competent as well as generally self-reliant. And it allows us to work less. Delegating responsibility to our children requires a foundation of love, shared values, and ready forgiveness as well as frequent communication.

When we come to grips with the practical aspect of mothering, we appreciate the many-layered significance and benefits of sound home management for our family and for the world at large. We also understand that, although we can do a lot as mothers, we cannot do everything. We therefore reduce our workload, delegate, acknowledge and respond to our physical, emotional, social, intellectual, and spiritual needs, and depend on God.

The larger the circle representing the aspect of mothering in the model of mothering, the more visible that aspect of mothering is to society. We cannot probe a mother's relationship to God, for example, but we can see her shopping for groceries. The four different aspects of mothering also differ dramatically in the extent to which they necessitate the involvement of others. The larger the circle representing the aspect of mothering in the model of mothering, the more people are required to assist a mother in her mothering. In believing, a mother depends on God and on the support of a spiritual advisor. In loving, a mother depends on support from her husband and her family and friends. In forgiving, a mother depends on support from a community that lives by and expresses a shared set of values. In persevering, a mother depends on a society and an economy that recognise, respect, and back her work in the home. By way of the mother's need for support, the different aspects of mothering involve an ever-widening circle of society in the task of mothering.

The different aspects of mothering also differ in the degree to which they can be delegated. The larger the circle representing the aspect of mothering in the model of mothering, the easier it is to delegate that aspect of mothering to others for some of the time without provoking a crisis in mothering. The spiritual aspect of mothering cannot be delegated. The emotional aspect of mothering requires primarily the commitment of the mother but also draws in her husband and other close family members as well as, possibly, friends who can be there for the baby. The social aspect of mothering, in turn, relies on the participation of many others. A mother cannot teach a moral framework by herself; she needs her husband and other adults as well as older children to take over from her from time to time the crucial task of communicating values to her children through word and deed. The practical aspect of mothering, lastly, can largely be delegated. The complete delegation of home-making activities to third parties, however, carries the risk that home life will become less expressive of the family's beliefs, loves, and values, and therefore less meaningful. It also carries the significant risk that children will not be taught to take on ever greater responsibility for themselves and others in the home, leaving them practically disabled. It is important, therefore, that a mother retain an influential and decisive role in home management even when she does not actually do most of the work herself, and that her children also remain involved in the work. Because the four aspects of mothering work together and complement one another, delegating entire aspects of mothering for long periods of time renders the job of mothering extremely difficult.

The different aspects of mothering, finally, tend to dominate mothering at different times. Before conception even and throughout pregnancy or while waiting to adopt, a mother considers her beliefs concerning mothering. When she finally holds her baby in her arms, she is consumed by the task of loving this little being. As her children grow and grow in independence, she takes care to pass on her values to them. And when she finds that she spots her nearly-grown children only occasionally on a given day, she concentrates on making sure that they are responsible and capable young people. Despite this shift in focus over the course of mothering, each aspect of mothering is important at each point in a child's life.

The four different aspects of mothering build on each other and give meaning to each other. Believing, and the submission to the divine will associated with believing, is a firm foundation for our loving because loving means more than feeling something: loving means commitment to a particular mode of conduct. We also need to experience God's unconditional love for us to help us to love our children unconditionally. Our authority as mothers, in turn, derives from our love for our children. It is because we give time to our children that we can share our values with our children. And it is because we can forgive our children that we can make demands on our children. The practical aspect of mothering, finally, embodies the other three. In persevering purposefully and prayerfully with our management of things and people in the home, we express and give substance to our beliefs, our love, and our values.

If we are experiencing difficulties within any one of the aspects of mothering, it can be helpful to focus our attention on the aspect of mothering immediately preceding that aspect in the model of mothering. Shifting our focus closer to the centre in this manner can lead us to the cause of the problems we are experiencing and therefore to their solution. Very simply and generally put: if you want your children to take on responsibility for themselves and others in the home and outside it, ensure you share your values with them. If you want your children to share your values, ensure you show them your love by being there for them. If you want to show your children your love by being there for them, ensure that you yourself feel loved and understand the implications of loving someone by turning to God.

Say, for instance, we want to teach our children to respect others. To accomplish this task in the social aspect of mothering, we need to provide the necessary foundation in the emotional aspect of mothering: we need to be there for our children. By being available, attentive, and responsive, we become confident in our role as mothers and in our understanding of our children. We also enjoy plenty of easy and pleasant times together with our children. In this way, being there for our children gives us both the competence and the opportunity to instruct our children in the values that matter to us through our conversation and example. Our children, in turn, are much more likely to try to live up to our values – rather than to rebel against them – when our attempts to teach them are backed up by our love for them.

While changes in the aspect of mothering represented by the next inner circle in the model of mothering are most likely to help us to overcome difficulties within an aspect of mothering, adjustments in any of the aspects of mothering can help since all the aspects of mothering work together. If we probe our *beliefs* regarding the value of respect, for instance, we can further define our understanding of respect by reference to the inherent dignity of the person created in the image of God. We can, in addition, ensure that our *home management* reflects our understanding of respect by purchasing fair trade goods, for example. In this way, our children will have a much fuller picture of the value of respect we are trying to communicate. By making changes in the emotional aspect of mothering and by integrating the spiritual and practical aspects of mothering into our undertaking, we can teach our children to respect others, and much else besides.

The model of mothering symbolised by the breast helps us to understand mothering as a holistic endeavour. The essential interrelatedness of the different aspects of mothering reflects the essential interrelatedness of the different dimensions of a person. Each aspect of mothering is backed up by and manifests the other aspects of mothering. Each aspect of mothering consequently involves our whole selves in our mothering our children as whole persons. When we understand mothering as a holistic endeavour, we realise that there are no short cuts in mothering – no short cuts, at any rate, that lead us and our children anywhere we want to be. When we understand mothering as a holistic endeavour, therefore, we are not tempted to adopt either of two increasingly common approaches to mothering: we are neither tempted to reduce our significance as mothers to that of glorified servants to our children nor are we tempted to reduce the significance of our children to that of inconveniences to be kept at bay. Although starkly contrasting, both of these approaches are similar in that both approaches reduce us as people. When we understand mothering as a holistic endeavour, we integrate our spiritual, emotional, social, and physical dimensions in our mothering and address and form the spiritual, emotional, social, and physical dimensions of our children through our mothering. And when we integrate our mothering, we know mothering to be a wholly satisfying undertaking. When we understand mothering as encompassing believing, loving, forgiving, and persevering, we rejoice both in our vocation as mothers and in our children's response to our mothering.

When we integrate our mothering, we are unlikely to harbour much doubt as to the value and meaning of our lives as we develop our and our children's whole selves in and through our mothering. This confidence in our vocation provides us with an antidote to the poison of employment-dependent identity squirted about so abundantly these days. Confidence in our vocation as mothers frees us from the need to prove our self-worth to ourselves and others with a suit and other trappings. It is not that employment is a bad thing, it is simply not the only thing. It isn't even the most important thing. By far. What, please, is this nonsense about work-life balance? Is it not clear that life has priority over work, not as 2 comes before 3 but as the oak tree has priority over the fungi clinging to it? Yes, there is a value judgment involved here but, being human, we cannot get around those. And, being human, we have to put life first. And, being human, moreover, living means loving or becomes meaningless.

As mothers fostering wholeness as we nourish life and love we represent the radical alternative to a fragmented society gone mad for the money, the kudos, and the more or less frivolous distractions money and kudos can buy. We also represent that society's hope.

Integrating mothering

We have seen that mothering is profoundly rewarding as well as profoundly important work. Good. Can mothers do it on their own? No.

Imagine a highly qualified teacher had been assigned a class to teach but that whenever she was about to start a lesson with her pupils, someone came in and asked her to help out and stock shelves at a supermarket or answer telephone calls at the travel agents'. Each time, our teacher dutifully reported to the other places of employment and the school secretary minded her class. All the while, moreover, the school around our teacher's pupils was being dismantled.

This is the situation of mothers in the United Kingdom. The government pays lip service to the crucial role of mothers in their children's upbringing while at the same time doing its level best to keep mothers away from their children by pushing them to work outside the home, to work full-time, as well as by arrogating the responsibilities of mothers.[7] Meanwhile, moreover, the government colludes in the dismantling of the one institution that provides the best context for mothers to work in and that has consistently been linked to better outcomes both for adults and their children: marriage.[8]

Imagine as well that the government's sole response to the increase in ill health in the population due to poor nutrition was to increase the number of general practitioners. It would have a case: more ill health therefore more doctors; the move would make sense from a certain perspective. But we all would almost certainly decry the action as quite beside the point, as falling far short of the government's responsibilities, because its intervention would be located too late in the chain of events to do much good.

This, however, is the government's approach to crises among Britain's children. The government applies elaborate sticking plasters where it could help to prevent the injury in the first place. It promotes programmes in schools to educate children about drugs, alcohol, and sex, and to warn them off antisocial behaviour and crime but neglects to support significantly the very people who – *given sufficient support* – could have the greatest possible lasting influence for good on children long before they reached school age[9]: the children's mothers.

Finally, imagine that Prince Charles' legs were of unequal length. Imagine further that the prince therefore ordered all the pavements in London to be made uneven so as to adjust for the discrepancy in his leg lengths and allow him to walk without limping. His problem, I dare say, would have been taken care of, albeit superficially, but the very solution to his problem would have caused significant problems for everybody who did not share it.

Now, the government's solutions to problems of mothering are of a similar order. Some children do not receive the stimulation they need at home, therefore the expansion of day-care is hailed as the best way forward for *all* children. Some children are physically abused, therefore *all* forms of physical correction is condemned.[10] Some children are brought up without a father, therefore the role of *all* fathers as supporters of and providers for the family is negated.[11] Some children cannot talk to their parents about sex, therefore *all* children are encouraged to seek confidential advice and information about contraceptives, sexually transmitted infections, and abortion from school nurses or sexual health clinics. Some children are neglected or abused by their parents, therefore *all* children and their parents' must come under state surveillance.[12] Legislation for the worst case is bad legislation as far as mothering is concerned because it significantly undermines the mothering which does not fall into the worst case category. A far more efficient use of resources would be for the government and its agencies to concentrate their efforts on those who have serious problems[13] and to *support*, rather than hassle and hinder, the majority who are quite willing and able to do right by their children.

By basing its policies on worst case scenarios – the incompetent mother, the absent father, the promiscuous teenager – the British government actually promotes an increase in worst cases. The government promotes incompetence in mothers by subsidising full-time childcare for very young children. Mothers cannot become competent mothers when they spend hardly any time with their children in their first few years of life.[14] The government promotes the absence of fathers by making mothers financially better off if they are lone parents rather than married to an unemployed man or to a man on a low income, as well as by doing away with the married couples' tax allowance and reducing widows' pensions. Removing financial incentives to marry and stay married increases the likelihood that children will not experience a stable family life and that mothers and their children will not benefit from the support and presence of fathers. The government promotes teenage promiscuity, finally, by making contraceptives freely available to teenagers, turning the use of contraceptives into the central issue of any discussion about sex[15], and by sidelining the influence of parents in shaping their children's attitudes to sex.

By making contraceptives easily available to ever younger children, the government, according to a study conducted by a team of economists from Nottingham University, actually causes the rates of unwanted teenage pregnancies and sexually transmitted infections to rise.[16] By severely neglecting the spiritual, moral, and emotional dimensions of sex in its sex education programmes, the government effectively cripples the ability of teenagers to appreciate any implications of sexual activity apart from the physical ones.[17] And by disregarding in its sex education strategy evidence showing that parents, especially mothers, are most teenagers' preferred source of advice and information about sex[18] and that parents, especially married parents[19], are far more successful than any school sex education programme in discouraging promiscuity among teenagers, the government further fails teenagers in this vitally important matter. The government, moreover, refuses to endorse abstinence education – which stresses the value of the gift of sexuality as well as the advantages of freedom from worries about pregnancy and infection – which is the *only* (!) sex education programme proven to lower teenage pregnancy rates and reduce the spread of sexually transmitted infections.[20] The government evidently takes it for granted that young teenagers are out of reach of their parents and sexually active (most, incidentally, are not[21]) and therefore concentrates on throwing condoms and abortifacient pills at them. This approach is certainly in the best interest of the contraceptive industry, it is not, however, in the best interest of teenagers.

Children need mothering, mothers and their children need the support and presence of the children's fathers, and children and their parents need the relative stability of marriage. Our mothering is inevitably flawed and the two-parent family is far from perfect and marriage is generally more of a challenging process than a blissful state, but they are the best options we have got, by a long shot. Mothering develops enduring relationships with children recognised as whole persons with individual needs and interests. Mothering communicates faith and hope, love and security, values and forgiveness to children and teaches children a sense of responsibility as well as necessary skills. Mothering, moreover, takes place primarily in the home where children learn to share their space, time, things, and selves with the people closest to them and to contribute to the on-going team effort that is the family. Mothering thus nurtures future spouses, parents, and neighbours as well as citizens and employees and is therefore infinitely superior to institutional methods of child-rearing which merely train future citizens and employees, if that. And the two-parent family based on a public, legal, and sacramental commitment of a man and a woman to each other for life provides a context in which mothers can mother without suffering undue strain because it promotes the inclusion of fathers. Rather than undermining mothers and the two-parent family and attempting to do their job for them – which it quite simply cannot do – the government must therefore support mothers and therefore fathers and therefore marriage. The government must help to enable mothers to do the best possible job that can be done so that children can be what they ought to be: happy and healthy, kind and conscientious, bright and capable.

What is needed is a change of heart among politicians. The evidence that mothering works and that two-parent families work is out there.[22] The evidence that what day-care centres, schools, sexual health clinics, social services, lone parent benefit, and various other institution-based government initiatives can achieve is *at the very best* only second best, is out there as well. But it will take a change of heart – a shift in ideologies – among politicians to enable them to see the evidence. Being politicians, the fact that *overwhelming popular support*, also among the young, for mothering, the family, and marriage is out there as well should eventually help to enhance their vision.[23]

What is to be done? Assuming politicians see the light, and surely they will, what can they do to help mothers to mother? Much needs to be done. Our political and economic system has to be remodelled to permit the optimal development of the child and the family: it has to be made to work for our future.[24] Here is an Action Plan:

- render full-time mothering of young children financially feasible for all mothers
- support mothers in their mothering
- integrate mothering into society.

Financing mothering. Most British mothers in employment (63 per cent) would like to work fewer hours and nearly half of all working mothers (44 per cent) would prefer to give up work altogether and stay at home with their children if they could afford to do so.[25] Another survey of 2,000 working mothers in Britain found that only one per cent would have chosen to return to full-time work after the birth of their baby, a third were happy to work part-time, but two-thirds said that they would rather be at home. Nearly all said that their relationships with their children had suffered.[26] Mothers evidently have been asking for bread and have been given stones: they have been asking for more time with their children and have been given subsidised institutionalised childcare. The majority of mothers are out at work not because they want to be but because they have to help pay the bills[27] – choice for most mothers as proffered by the government is limited to the choice to leave their children in a stranger's care. Ultimately, of course, society pays the bill for the children the mothers cannot mother. It is time to provide bread.

There evidently is plenty of money in the pot, only its distribution is rot.[28] Here are some suggestions for using large sums of money to give mothers what they actually want rather than what the government says they want, ways of using money to enable mothers to mother: 1. Allowing a mother who mainly mothers to transfer her unused personal tax allowance to her husband is a start. 2. Income splitting, which is the norm in several European countries, is better still: a family income is split into two halves to calculate the tax rate for each spouse. 3. In addition, a child tax allowance reflecting the extra costs and responsibilities of having dependent children would give parents real choice as it allows parents to decide themselves whether to use the money saved in tax to allow the mother or father to stay at home or to pay others – family, friends, or professionals – to look after their children. (Most mothers, who require childcare, incidentally, prefer informal or family-based childcare to institutionalised childcare![29]) All three measures require much less bureaucratic input and offer parents much greater freedom and flexibility than a system of subsidised childcare in day-care centres. The measures have the further virtue of encouraging joint decision-making in couples by treating them as a unit.[30]

How will the government pay for any of this? Research suggests that divorce rates along with their associated costs for the government will decrease when fewer mothers do double duty in a full-time job as well as at home.[31] The government will, moreover, make enormous savings as the costs of diet-related poor health, behavioural and learning difficulties, pregnancies, anti-social behaviour, delinquency, and substance abuse among the young plummet and as increasing numbers of bright and capable youngsters enter employment and become tax payers.[32] Mothers invest in their children. The government would do well to invest in mothers.

Supporting mothering. Greater job mobility and long working hours mean that most mothers these days have neither the previous relevant experience nor the easily accessible support that living near the extended family can provide and, moreover, have to manage without much day-to-day help from their husbands. In addition, with many mothers forced out to work, there is little opportunity for mothers to build up emotional and practical support networks with other mothers in the same neighbourhood. Children along with their mothers bear the brunt of these economic and political pressures. They sense their mothers' insecurity in their mothering. They suffer under their mothers' stress from overwork. Herded into full-time day-care, moreover, they learn all about colours and numbers but very little about loving and living. They are deprived of what they need: care and attention from their parents, real-life adult role models, home-cooked meals, unstructured time spent outside and in the home with friends or family, the chance to observe adult interaction and adults at work. And given too much of what they do not need: computers, gadgets, TV, microwaved ready-meals, car journeys, structured time spent in institutions in large groups, segregated children's environments. Women still become mothers, children still grow up – but the rug is being pulled from underneath them. It is difficult for mothers to mother well and for children to grow up good when both are struggling for support.

I expect that politicians on the whole know that it is mothers and families rather than day-care centres and schools who can do the best possible job bringing up children. The problem for politicians is, I suspect, that they do not know that mothers and families *will* do the best possible job bringing up children. Mothers and families, unlike day-care centres and schools, are frightfully impervious to quality control. However, as any experienced mother could tell the concerned politicians, you cannot control people anyway, no matter how many controls you put in place. If, like a good mother, you are interested in *results* rather than controls, your best bet is to give people guidance and support and to hold them accountable[33] – and the key factor here is support. This is as true for mothers and families as it is true for teachers, doctors, academics and other professionals.[34] Instead of funding elaborate control structures – and much of what runs in the UK under childcare and children's rights[35] is essentially that – which don't do much good, funding support structures for mothers and families would do a world of good.

Mothers need many different kinds of support in their mothering. Here are some ways of giving mothers that support: 1. Antenatal mothering courses should become a matter of course, as integral to any pregnancy as childbirth classes have become. Pregnant women in particularly difficult circumstances should have access to individual sessions with a specially trained midwife or counsellor. 2. Mothers of special needs children should receive the support their children need as soon as the special need is diagnosed rather than have to wait as well as to fight for that support as is all too frequently the case.[36] Given the hyperabundance which marks our society, failure to provide adequately for our society's weakest members marks our society a failure. 3. While networks of first-time mothers are helpful they are not as helpful as links to mothers with perspective gained from experience. Mentoring could help first-time mothers through the anxiety-ridden first few weeks or months of mothering. First-time mothers would be matched up and then meet regularly with trained experienced mothers both before and after the birth of their child for as long as they felt the need for reassurance, help, and advice. Social Services would pay for the mothers' mentors' services. 4. Subsidised home-help for mothers of babies would help to give mothers and their children a better start. 5. Weekend retreats for mothers of children of all ages would be enjoyed by everyone in the family. The mother would enjoy time away, meals prepared by someone else, and the opportunity to think and learn more about her mothering together with other mothers, the father would enjoy home rule and his children, and the children would enjoy their father.

The government must furthermore and perhaps most importantly recognise and endorse marriage as a vital pillar of support for mothers and their children. A policy of endorsing marriage would be comparable to the existing policy of endorsing formal education. The government endorses formal education because formal education has been proven to promote children's long-term welfare. By the same token, the government should endorse marriage because marriage has been proven to promote children's long-term welfare: having married parents has been unequivocally linked to better outcomes for children's physical, emotional, mental, social, and educational development. Endorsing formal education does not imply that people who missed out on formal education are morally inferior or that it is impossible to succeed in life without a formal education. Endorsing marriage would neither imply that mothers who are not married are morally inferior nor that they cannot succeed as mothers. Endorsing marriage, like endorsing formal education, is not a moral judgment – it is a strategy to improve dramatically the life chances of our nation's children.

I have already discussed several ways of endorsing marriage by means of taxation. In addition, the benefits system needs to be restructured so as to allow a married man to support his wife and children, as is the case in France and Germany. Higher pension benefits for widows should be restored as well. Financial incentives to marry and stay married pay for themselves as greater family stability lowers the costs of social disruption.[37] Marriage preparation courses, moreover, need to become much more widely available – with fewer and fewer of us having had the opportunity to observe a marriage in action as children, we need all the help we can get.[38] In addition, abstinence education should be introduced in schools not only to reduce teenage pregnancy rates but also to promote the concept of marriage among school children.

Marriage matters because fathers matter. Fathers matter as emotional, practical, social, and financial supporters of mothers. Fathers matter as nurturing and guiding parents of their children. Fathers matter as models of masculinity to their children – as examples of what it means to be a man – and as such help their sons and daughters to find their own places in society.[39] And fathers matter as one half of a couple because together with their wives they teach their children about respect and concern, self-giving and commitment, conflict and conflict resolution in marriage – profound lessons children need for the future.[40] Being a father is a vocation which deserves support in its own right. Fathers need several weeks of paid paternity leave with cover for their jobs included in the deal (else, as in the case of my husband's recent joke of a two-week paternity leave, they will probably work at their jobs from home to the extent possible) so that they can give full-time support to their wives in that crucial period after the birth of a child as well as bond with their babies themselves. Parenting courses for fathers of older children would also help to put fathers back to where they are needed most: in their families. A health centre in Stockport runs such a course in a pub. Good for them! Above all, however, excessively long working hours must be curbed so that working fathers as well as working mothers are free to spend more time at home.[41] We need to work to make efficiency and effectiveness – not busyness and burn-out – characterise working culture in Britain. I am sure it can be done. Legislation could be a start.

Integrating mothering. For an increasing number of people, men as well as women, work doesn't work any more.[42] Long hours are damaging their health and their relationships[43], and job satisfaction among women has been declining over the past fifteen years; they are now as disillusioned as men.[44] Women fought for the opportunity to join the men's world of work on the men's terms only to discover a generation or two down the line, that the fight hadn't been altogether worth it. Like men, women had come to expect self-fulfilment through work and were disappointed. Confined to the home in the 1950s, women found themselves confined to the office or the shop floor in the 1990s, which imposed its own limitations on who they could be. It is not work itself, however tedious, which is the problem. The problem is our modern conviction that it is primarily work which defines who we are. A work-based definition of who we are will always and necessarily be unsatisfactory – jobs simply aren't that fulfilling. The terms under which we work, however, leave us little choice but to seek self-fulfilment through what we do for a living rather than through living. Work today requires us to relegate the relationships that give most meaning to our existence, our family relationships, to the margins of that existence. Career structures, for example, discourage women from having children and render them apologetic about it when they do, and working hours make it well nigh impossible for parents to raise their own children. The separation of, to use current terminology, work and life in our society proceeds at the expense of the latter: life is segregated; it is the mildly risible, embarrassing outsider to the central business of working.

As a result of the segregation of life, ignorance about children prevails in our society and child-rearing practices, in turn, further underpin the segregation of life. Day-care centres and extended school hours effectively remove children from public sight and awareness. Driving rather than walking, cycling, or using public transport with children has the same effect – extensive car use renders children invisible. The minimal provision of communal spaces in our cities isolates mothers and their children in their homes and therefore inhibits the spontaneous sharing of childcare with neighbours which is commonplace elsewhere in the world. The convention that children eat separately from adults and, moreover, eat special children's food (and, here is what really irks me: eat without any table manners) is another segregating child-rearing practice which, I am pleased to note, has actually not caught on in many societies outside the UK. As a practice, it confines the mother and her children to a separate domain from which the mother can, to be sure, emerge on occasion, but only once she has stripped off her motherhood. And then there is breastfeeding. It is utterly astounding that, after decades of feminism, breastfeeding in public continues to be a hotly debated issue in the West. Nursing mothers who dare not breastfeed in public – and, yes, it still takes daring to do so – are needlessly cut off from much of society.

Another and final example of Western child-rearing practices that tend to confer an outsider status on mothers is the widespread use of prams. Do, for a minute, consider the effect of prams on the mobility of the mother. When you are pushing a huge and heavy vehicle around with you, where can you go? And how fast can you get there? And how much effort will it take you to get there? And is that effort worth it? And how many people will you in-convenience by the space your vehicle takes up? The Western invention of prams limits mothers in a multitude of ways. Most women around the world carry their babies on their backs – so you definitely don't have to be a Valkyrie to do so. Carrying your baby on your back renders you as mobile as the next person (and does, incidentally, fight osteoporosis while you are at it as carrying babies is weight-bearing exercise). With your baby on your back, moreover, you are much more likely to be seen as a person in your own right; when pushing a pram, mothers are typically dismissed as adjuncts to a role.[45] And prams, of course, are merely the tip of the iceberg of stuff considered essential equipment in Western society for bringing up children, stuff which renders mothering not only expensive but also an unwieldy and inflexible and therefore isolating activity. The segregation of life thus reproduces itself: children do not fit in with our work, ergo they are tucked away, ergo ignorance about children continues to prevail, ergo the terms of our work remain the same. This has got to change, for everybody's sake.

The most immediate way of bringing about the de-segregation of life is to integrate mothering into society. Life doesn't come more risible and embarrassing, no more extraneous to the business of working, than in the guise of mothering. When we integrate mothering into society, therefore, we let life in. We integrate life in all its laughable, embarrassing, immeasurable, demanding, rewarding, and incredibly joyful unpredictability. And when we let life in, the quality of life goes up for everybody.

Let us raise our children in families, neighbourhoods, and communities, not in segregated institutions – so that our children grow up to be fit for families, neighbourhoods, and communities, not segregated institutions! Let us demand working conditions across the board that leave plenty of time and energy for mothers together with fathers and friends and family and neighbours to mother children. Job-shares, part-time work, flexible working hours, and the option of working from home some or much of the time need to become the rule rather than the exception.[46] Maternity pay, moreover, needs to be drawn from a central fund to which employers contribute in proportion to their number of employees, male and female, to prevent discrimination against women in hiring practice.[47] We need mothers in the work force because of their skills and experience and because they help us to keep life in the picture. Let us see open days for families at our places of work, family-friendly events organised by employers, and family-support services provided by employers. Let us see baby changing facilities for use by men as well as women in all public places and more pubs and restaurants welcoming families and serving children as well as adults decent food. Let us see schools, clubs, and churches involve adults of different backgrounds in teaching children about work and life skills and faith. Let us see housing developments that provide central, enclosed communal gardens and architecture that encourages extended families to live together. Let us see designated play roads in every neighbourhood, strictly enforced 20-mph speed limits in residential areas, and 'walking buses' to schools that pick up all the children in an area.[48] Let us see every business, organisation, and neighbourhood fit for the family!

Integrating mothering into society effects an exchange of skills, experience, and perspectives between mothers and society. When we integrate mothering into society, a mother is well and truly included in society and enabled to take an active part in it through paid work and other activities even as she devotes much of her time to mothering. When we integrate mothering into society, moreover, mothering becomes a more inclusive activity. The mother is not left alone to bear the burdens and enjoy the joys of mothering; she has the father, friends, and relatives by her side and enjoys significant and practical community support. Child psychologist Steve Biddulph notes that "a caring, close neighbourhood does far more to prevent child abuse (through its removal of loneliness and boredom) than any number of doctors and social workers. [...] When families are woven in with friends and neighbours, and when people of all generations have access to each other, then we won't need psychologists or departments of social welfare. We'll take care of ourselves."[49] Integrating mothering into society therefore benefits society at least as much as it benefits mothers.

When mothering is integrated into society, the value of mothers as well as their needs are generally recognised.

Mothers therefore embark on mothering both informed and supported. Teenagers are given plenty of opportunity to have a go at mothering their younger siblings and the young children of neighbours, relatives, and friends of their parents. They also have countless occasions to observe all sorts of people engage in mothering in all sorts of ways and to listen to them discuss the pains and pleasures of mothering – and because they know mothering to be an important and difficult occupation, they pay attention. In addition, the popular media[50] and school lessons provide them with mothering role models. The birth of a baby is a cause of joy for everybody in the parents' circle of friends and relations, and everyone is able to make time to rally round to cook and clean and cuddle and adore and give advice which the parents can ignore. As children grow up, moreover, they have several trusted adult figures in their lives to emulate and confide in and learn from and argue with, in addition to a mother and a father who are thoroughly involved in family life as well as engaged in work and interests outside the home. Children, moreover, learn from being integrated *as children* in adult activities: they learn to be attentive and obedient when observing or assisting with adult activities and thereby learn about the values and the work of adults which prepares them well for taking on greater responsibilities of their own.[51] Mothers feel glad and proud to be mothers, knowing that their mothering as well as their children are widely and deeply appreciated.

When we integrate mothering into society, children are no longer segregated for most of the day in more or less appropriate child-specific environments but able to form an impression of society directly and to be active in it. When we integrate mothering into society, children therefore learn a lot more a lot more quickly. They learn about their obligations to others and others' needs. They learn about social interaction and the beliefs and the norms that sustain it. They learn about the time and the discipline required to do a job well and the satisfaction gained from doing a job well. When we integrate mothering into society, moreover, children enjoy a higher standard of living. When children share meals with their parents, for example, they are much more likely to enjoy freshly cooked food than when they are fed separately, they are also much more likely to enjoy conversations with their parents. In addition, children enjoy more opportunities to relax when mothering is integrated into society as well as much more scope for developing their imagination and their initiative. They enjoy greater freedom of movement and the chance to explore their natural environment. Instead of being cooped up in a car and then confined to the nursery or school for the entire day, children enjoy the time and the space to rest as well as to play their own games and to climb and swing and balance and throw and kick and hide and seek in the sun and in the rain and beneath the trees and by the pond: they enjoy the freedom to be children, which alone will proof them for life against temptations to childishness. And it is men and women who have learned all this and enjoyed all this whom society needs above all.

Integration

Mothering almost inevitably effects a reconfiguration of a woman's values. A well-supported mother learns to put her children's needs before her own and is rewarded with the profound joy that attends such self-giving. When we give mothering the place it deserves at the centre of society, mothering will similarly effect a reconfiguration of society's values. When we begin to base policies on the needs of mothers and children, mothering will change society from the centre outward – and the flow of benefits from mothering to society will be immense.

Mothering is the penultimate case of self-giving (the ultimate being martyrdom), on a par with living the vows of obedience, poverty, and chastity. It is also a quite wonderful way of self-realisation which is, after all, only achieved through "a sincere gift of self"[52], and in this respect again, I suspect, comparable to monastic life. But the thing about mothering is that you can involve other people in it, that you can share its blessings in a direct and immediate manner. The love between mother and child is something at once intimate and potentially inclusive.[53] And well-loved children inevitably share the love they know wherever they go. When we take mothering out of the confines of the home and into society, therefore, we not only share the work of mothering we also share the joys of mothering. And with the work as well as the joys of mothering we share the gospel of self-giving: we share our commitment to nurture life and to persevere in love as well as the good news that giving ourselves to life and love blesses us with life and love. People can only cherish what they know. Through sharing the work and the joys of mothering, we can help others to appreciate the infinite value of life and love and therefore the value of self-giving, and so humanise society and generate a true culture of life, a culture full of joy.

There it is then, my vision of a bright future for mothers and children and for society: a transformation, no less, of our culture so that it supports life.[54] When mothers integrate their mothering and mothering is integrated into society, we can wholly embrace life and love and reverse this restless fragmentation. We can find serenity, meaning, and joy as we ourselves become whole, both as individuals and as a society. And when we are whole, we are not far from holiness.

So let us suffer no false humility. "We are born to manifest the glory of God that is within us!"[55] Every mother is called through her mothering to let the concentric circles of faith, love, forgiveness, and perseverance radiate far beyond her home. Humanity depends on it.

1 One-hundred and ten eminent childcare experts signed a letter to *The Daily Telegraph* which stated that "consistent, continuous care by a trusted figure is the key to providing a secure and nurturing environment for very young children" and that "research suggests that its absence can lead to emotional difficulties," *The Daily Telegraph*, 21 October 2006.

2 'Hidden stress of the nursery age', *The Guardian*, 19 September 2005, referring to a study by Michael Lamb of Cambridge University.

3 'Kluge Koepfchen', *Focus*, 4 March 1996.

4 See, for instance, 'After-school clubs may pose threat to emotional growth', *The Times*, 6 January 2006 and F. Smith and J. Barker, 'Contested spaces: Children's experiences of out of school care in England and Wales', *Childhood*, 7(3), 2000: 315–333.

5 Jill Kirby, *The Price of Parenthood* (Centre for Policy Studies, 2004).

6 Harry Benson, 'The conflation of marriage and cohabitation in government statistics – a denial of difference rendered untenable by an analysis of outcomes', Bristol Community Family Trust, September 2006, *http://www.bcft.co.uk/research.htm*

7 The UK government's 'overarching strategy for all children and young people from conception to age 19' with its attendant targets and frameworks implies that the state has the primary responsibility for the upbringing of children, see Jill Kirby, *The Nationalisation of Childhood* (London: Centre for Policy Studies, 2006) p. 48.

8 Numerous studies conducted by various bodies have linked marriage to better physical and mental health in the couple, lower incidence of domestic violence, and better performance at school as well a lower incidence of drug use, alcohol abuse, antisocial behaviour, sexual activity, running away from home, and pregnancy among the children of married couples. See, for example, Patricia Morgan, *Marriage-Lite: The Rise of Cohabitation and its Consequences* (London: Civitas, 2000). A recent UK study, moreover, conclusively shows that marriage provides a far more stable environment for the raising of children than unmarried families even after other factors such as age, income, education, and ethnicity are taken into account, cf. Harry Benson, 'The conflation of marriage and cohabitation in government statistics – a denial of difference rendered untenable by an analysis of outcomes', Bristol Community Family Trust, September 2006, *http://www.bcft.co.uk/research.htm*

9 "...for a boy is only sent to be taught at school when it is too late to teach him anything. The real thing has been done already, and

thank God it is nearly always done by women", G.K. Chesterton, *Orthodoxy* (London: Hodder & Stoughton, 1996) p. 232.

10 No, I am not a proponent of smacking. I am, however, an opponent of the removal of parents from their children because they have smacked them. A father in Manchester, for example, was barred from living with his partner and their three-year-old son and new-born baby daughter for six months because he had been spotted by a policeman administering a forceful smack to his son's bottom just after the boy had run into the road, *Manchester Metro News*, 10 December 2004.

11 The trend, to be fair, predates the present government in Britain. See, for example, Norman Dennis, George Erdos, *Families without Fatherhood* (London: Civitas, 1992). For a more recent take on the subject, see Melanie Phillips, *The sex-change society* (The Social Market Foundation, 1999).

12 "'When you are looking for a needle in a haystack, is it necessary to keep building bigger haystacks?' said Jonathan Bamford, assistant commissioner at the Commissioner's office which promotes access to official information and the protection of personal information. Keeping check on 11 million or 12 million children, when the justification for the database was that three or four million were in some way 'at risk', was 'not proportionate', he said," *The Daily Telegraph*, 26 June 2006.

13 As, for instance, in Michigan where the Perry Pre-school programme helps children as well as their parents who are finding it difficult to cope, see Patricia Morgan, *Who Needs Parents?*, IEA, 1996.

14 According to Jay Belsky, Professor of Psychology at the Institute for the Study of Children, Families and Social Issues, at Birkbeck College, University of London, the more time a child spends in day-care during the first two or three years of his life, the less sensitive mothering he is likely to receive and the less harmonious the mother-child relationship will be, cf. *FYC Family Bulletin*, Summer 2006.

15 I consider it a great pity that adults generally come across to teenagers as having nothing more important to say about sex than "use a condom".

16 "The study, led by David Paton, used data from 95 health authorities in England and Wales to reveal that such problems [as unwanted teenage pregnancies and sexually transmitted diseases] were more acute in precisely the areas where the Government's sexual health strategy had been most actively pursued," *The Catholic Herald*, 9 April 2004. There will be several reasons for this. For one, the introduction of a safety device, in this case contraceptives, frequently prompts people to take greater risks. For another, condoms do not

actually provide protection against most sexually transmitted infections.

17 Few teenagers are, for instance, prepared for the psychological consequences of sexual activity, cf. Dr Trevor Stammers, 'Sexual Spin', *Postgraduate Medical Journal*, September 1999. Lynette Burrows describes "the whole slant of current sex-education" in Britain as "mechanical, ugly, dangerous and middle-aged", *The Catholic Herald*, 1 February 2002.

18 *FYC Family Bulletin*, Autumn 1999.

19 Children from broken homes are twice as likely to be sexually active as children living with both parents, cf. Clifford Hill, *Sex under Sixteen?* (London: Family Education Trust, 2000).

20 In the USA and Uganda, cf. T.G. Stammers, 'Abstinence under fire', *FYC Family Bulletin*, Autumn 2003,
see also Fred Naylor, *The Family Way: The Case for Abstinence Education* (Campaign for Real Education)

21 Only 17 per cent were sexually active among a cohort of over 2000 teenagers aged 13-15, according to a survey conducted by the Family Education Trust in September 2000.

22 Need more convincing? Read the books by the child psychologists Steve Biddulph, Penelope Leach, and Daniel N. Stern, consider the findings of Professor Jay Belsky, Director of the Institute for the Study of Children, Families and Social Issues at London University's Birkbeck College, that, *regardless of the quality of the childcare*, "children who spent more time in childcare during their first five years scored lower on a composite measure of positive adjustment (i.e. peer popularity, teacher-rated peer competence) and higher on a composite measure of negative adjustment (i.e. teacher-rated behaviour problems, peer dislike, observed aggression) than children with less childcare experience" (Jay Belsky, 'Developmental Risks (Still) Associated with Early Child Care', *Journal of Child Psychology and Psychiatry*, 2001) as well as the results of a study carried out by Professor Kathy Sylva of Oxford University following the progress of 3,000 children in the UK which indicated that under-twos who spent long hours in daycare were more likely to be anti-social when they start school (Sylva, Melhuish, et al, *The Effective Provision of Pre-School Education Project*, Institute of Education, University of London, 2003), re-read endnote number 8 to this chapter describing the positive impact of marriage on parents and their children, and listen to Jack Straw, the then Home Secretary, who, on the Today Programme on 4 November 1998 stated: "Children in my judgment, and I think it's the judgment of almost everyone including single parents, are best brought up where you have two natural parents in a stable relationship. There's

no question about that. What we know from the evidence is that, generally speaking, that stability is more likely to occur where the parents are married than where they are not."

23 Sociological research confirms that "[...] for most women motherhood remains central to their identity and is a positive experience (Ruddick 1980; McMahon 1995; Benn 1998); and that communities as well as individual families lose something from the trend towards dual-earner households that leaves residential neighbourhoods empty by day (Etzioni 1993a, 1993b)", cf. Catherine Hakim, *Work-Lifestyle Choices in the 21st Century* (Oxford: Oxford University Press, 2000): 235. Most people think that marriage is a good thing, and most young people hope to get married one day, cf. survey results cited in 'Traditional Family' *FYC Family Bulletin,* Winter 1999/2000 and in Clifford Hill, *Sex under Sixteen?* (London: Family Education Trust, 2000). The majority of people, moreover, prefer marriages with different roles for husband and wife, cf. Catherine Hakim, *Work-Lifestyle Choices in the 21st Century* (Oxford: Oxford University Press, 2000). See also the survey results mentioned in the next paragraph but one in the text.

24 "It is shameful that our political and economic system does not support the optimal development of the child and family," Daniel N. Stern, Nadia Bruschweiler-Stern, Alison Freeland, *The Birth of a Mother: How motherhood changes you forever* (London: Bloomsbury, 1998) p. 173.

25 Figures cited in a UK government document entitled *Choice for Parents: The Best Start for Children,* published by the Treasury in December 2004.

26 'Working mothers demand choice to stay at home', *The Daily Telegraph,* 8 January 2004.

27 According to sociologist Catherine Hakim, "Most mothers prefer to care for their young children themselves. [...] financial considerations rather than a strong personal commitment to paid work, are often the prime motivation for mothers' return to employment soon after childbirth", Catherine Hakim, *Work-Lifestyle Choices in the 21st Century* (Oxford: Oxford University Press, 2000) p. 234. For another detailed account of *what women want* see Jill Kirby, *Choosing to be Different* (London: Centre for Policy Studies, 2003).

28 The UK government recently earmarked another £769 million for institutionalised childcare, for example, *The Daily Telegraph,* 15 February 2006.

29 S. Vegris, *Childcare for child development or childcare for mothers' work? Some evidence from the Families and Children Study* (FACS), Policy Studies Institute, 2004.

30 Catherine Hakim makes this point, and also draws attention to a "side-effect of the Swedish [tax] system [which] is to make spouses' work decisions independent of each other and thus to facilitate and encourage separation and divorce, since individuals already function as separate financial units anyway," Catherine Hakim, *Work-Lifestyle Choices in the 21st Century* (Oxford: Oxford University Press, 2000): 228.

31 Professor Carey Cooper of the (then) University of Manchester Institute of Science and Technology's School of Management: "We [in the UK] have the highest divorce rate in Europe. I don't think it's unrelated [to long working hours] in that two out of three couples are working couples," *Metro*, 28 October 1999. A recent study by Professor Susan MacRae of Oxford Brookes University, moreover, reports that mothers who return to work full-time soon after having had a baby are much more likely to end up divorced than those who stay at home or work part-time, cf. Jill Kirby, *Choosing to be Different* (London: Centre for Policy Studies, 2003) p. 20. Overall, there is a greater incidence of divorce in households where mothers are in full-time work, ibid. 43. A conservative estimate of the cost of divorce is £4.5 billion a year (*British Vogue*, October 1997).

32 "Supporting young mothers and fathers to have more time is good economics, in preventing socially dysfunctional young people from filling our schools, streets, and work places of the future. We need people who are calm, caring, able to bond and be close. We are breeding the very opposite", child psychologist Steve Biddulph, quoted in *The Daily Telegraph*, 21 October 2006.

33 Accountability backed by support works. In Holland, for example, girls who get pregnant are the financial responsibility of their parents (=accountability), many more mothers than in the UK can and do stay at home (=support for mothering) where they share values, meals, and chores with their children (=mothering), and teenage pregnancy rates in Holland are very low. There you go. (Only 20% of women in the Netherlands are in full-time employment; Dutch women are entitled to maintenance and social welfare via their dependence on their husbands, cf. Catherine Hakim, *Work-Lifestyle Choices in the 21st Century* (Oxford: Oxford University Press, 2000) p. 57.) For a detailed study of the Dutch situation, see Joost van Loon, *Deconstructing the Dutch Utopia: Sex education and teenage pregnancy in the Netherlands* (London: Family Education Trust, 2003).

34 I have an axe to grind: when I was running a church playgroup in a decrepit community hall my staff and I who did the important work with the children were paid a small wage by the hour while a

seemingly endless stream of salaried and pensioned men and women in suits passed through, sitting around drinking our coffee, keeping an eye on us, and leaving behind countless expensively produced slogan-slinging publications telling us what we already knew, as well as stacks of paperwork for me. As mentioned before: there clearly is plenty of money in the pot, only its distribution is rot!

35 Dr Eileen Munro from the Department of Social Policy at the London School of Economics, for instance, argued at a conference held on 27 June 2006 at the London School of Economics that the current government's plans for increased official surveillance of children indicated a suspicious attitude towards parents and a shift away from parents and towards local children's services to ensure that the basic needs of children were met, cf. *FYC Family Bulletin*, Summer 2006. And Margaret Morrissey of the National Confederation of Parent Teacher Associations said on the BBC News on 9 November 2005 that "we are now in danger of taking away children's childhood when they leave the maternity ward. From the minute you are born and your parents go back to work, as the government has encouraged them to do, you are going to be ruled by the Department of Education." See also Jill Kirby, *The Nationalisation of Childhood* (London: Centre for Policy Studies, 2006) for a thorough and cogent assessment of the evidence indicating that this government is intent "to oversee, influence, and (ultimately) control the upbringing of children" (op. cit., p. 45).

36 Support from the state for disabled children and their families is extremely poor. "[…] parents struggle to even obtain a wheelchair for their child, let alone someone to help put them to bed at night or offer occasional respite care. A survey by the Downing Street Strategy Unit of 3,000 parents of disabled children found that 77 per cent could not access basic equipment such as beds and hoists. The charity Mencap warns that thousands of people are at breaking point over the lack of financial and emotional support available […]. There is not enough funding, services are disjointed and the system is too inflexible, according to a report published earlier this month by the Birth Defects Foundation," *The Independent*, 19 October 2006.

37 "[…] It is an uncomfortable fact that children born outside conventional family structures tend to place a greater strain on the State in due course. Their levels of academic and economic achievement are lower, their propensity to commit crime higher," *The Times*, 19 August 2001.

38 In counties in the United States which have a Community Marriage Policy involving local clergy and voluntary organisations providing

marriage preparation as well as mentoring and support programmes for troubled marriages, divorce rates are declining nearly twice as fast as in comparison counties, cf. Jill Kirby, *The Price of Parenthood* (London, Centre for Policy Studies, 2005) pp. 38-39. In a long-term study, engaged couples who went through the Prevention and Relationship Enhancement Program developed at the University of Denver (PREP) were half as likely to divorce than couples who did not (*British Vogue*, October 1997). In the UK, Marriage Care offers marriage preparation courses as well as counselling for couples, see www.marriagecare.org.uk tel. (020) 7371 1341, or Scottish Marriage Care (0141) 222 2166. Books can also help, e.g Ed Wheat, *Love life for every married couple.*

39   Through rough play, for example, fathers teach their children, in particular their sons, how to enjoy as well as to control their physical strength. An important lesson, clearly. By treating their daughters with love and respect, moreover, fathers help their daughters to develop greater self-esteem. Low self-esteem among girls is associated with significantly greater risk of teenage pregnancy, cf. N. Emler, *Self-esteem: the costs and causes of low self-worth* (Joseph Rowntree Foundation, 2001).

40   James Stenson makes this point in the second chapter of his excellent book *Upbringing* (Princeton, N.J.: Scepter, 1991).

41   "...The British experience of work is getting worse, with more people saying they don't spend enough time at home", *Metro,* 28 October 1999.

42   Elizabeth Perle McKenna, *When work doesn't work anymore* (London: Simon & Schuster, 1997)

43   *Metro,* 28 October 1999.

44   'Women are no longer happy in their work, says study', *The Daily Telegraph,* 28 June 2005.

45   I am indebted to Anna Carver for drawing my attention to this phenomenon.

46   House prices, that popular justification for our work-centred culture, will adjust to an *overall* change in income levels.

47   "More than 60 per cent of company directors surveyed by NOP say they are reluctant to hire young women because of the heavy weight imposed by the Government's maternity regulations", *The Sunday Telegraph,* 6 April 2003.

48   There goes a sacred cow. A cliché holds that a mother who does the school run is a good mother. Far better, I say, to do away with the school run and let your children walk and talk with other children, see the world and be seen by it, and experience the elements on their way to and from school! In Germany, the popular media help to educate primary school children about road safety every summer.

You could contact www.school-run.org to find out whether there is a 'walking bus' scheme in your area. Children (and adults!) who walk or cycle, incidentally, are exposed to significantly lower levels of pollutants than those travelling by a car.

49 Steve Biddulph, *The Secret of Happy Children* (London: Thorsons: Thorsons, 1998) pp. 134, 138.

50 Have you noticed how magazines for girls and young women, even the less trashy ones that try to stimulate interest in careers, do not discuss the one activity most of their readers are likely to be involved in before long? Apart from the occasional shocker about a teenager mother, mothering is not mentioned in these publications.

51 The children in a village in Ghana where I worked in the summer of 1985 were quite marvellous. Their presence was accepted everywhere because they knew how to behave in different contexts: they were playful at play and attentive and obedient when an adult, any adult, in the village asked them to fetch a bucket of water, for instance, and quietly observant in church or when attending the council of elders. Due to the segregation of mothering and therefore of children in our society, British children hardly get a chance to develop such a refined register of appropriate behaviours nor, which is worse, do they get much chance to learn by observing and assisting adults engaged in adult activities.

52 Cf. John Paul II, *Mulieris Dignitatem*, p. 7.

53 I can, for example, say to a friend, "Isn't he gorgeous, would you like a cuddle?" when I am referring to our toddler but not – better not – if I am referring to my husband.

54 John Paul II, *Evangelium Vitae.*

55 Nelson Mandela in his inaugural address, cited in Fr Ronald Rolheiser, 'Real and false humility', *The Catholic Herald.*